Why Does Language Matter to Philosophy?

to Philosophy?

Ian Hacking

D0147865

Cambridge University Press

Cambridge
London • New York • Melbourne

Published by the Syndics of the Cambridge University Press
The Pitt Building, Trumpington Street, Cambridge CB2 1RP
Bentley House, 200 Euston Road, London NW1 2DB
32 East 57th Street, New York, NY 10022, USA
296 Beaconsfield Parade, Middle Park, Melbourne 3206, Australia

© Cambridge University Press 1975

Library of Congress Catalogue Card Number: 75–19432

ISBN 0 521 20923 4 hard covers
ISBN 0 521 09998 6 paperback

First published 1975

Type set by Radnor Graphic Arts, Philadelphia, Pennsylvania; printed
in the United States of America by R. R. Donnelley & Sons Company,
Crawfordsville, Indiana

Why Does Language Matter to Philosophy?

For Jane Frances

Contents

Preface   vii

  1 Strategy   1

A. The heyday of ideas

  2 Thomas Hobbes' mental discourse   15
  3 Port Royal's ideas   26
  4 Bishop Berkeley's abstractions   34
  5 Nobody's theory of meaning   43

B. The heyday of meanings

  6 Noam Chomsky's innatism   57
  7 Bertrand Russell's acquaintance   70
  8 Ludwig Wittgenstein's articulation   82
  9 A. J. Ayer's verification   93
10 Norman Malcolm's dreams   103

C. The heyday of sentences

11 Paul Feyerabend's theories   115
12 Donald Davidson's truth   129
    I. Tarski's theory 130   II. Problems and extensions
    134   III. The theory of meaning 140   IV. The veri-
    fication of T-sentences 144 V. Charity and hu-
    manity 146   VI. The determinacy of translation 150

13 Why does language matter to philosophy?   157
    A. The heyday of ideas 163   B. The heyday of mean-
    ings 170   C. The heyday of sentences 177

Bibliography   188
Index   197

Preface

This book comes from a course of lectures first given in Cambridge in the Easter Term of 1972 and repeated, in a revised and augmented form, in Michaelmas 1973. Quite a lot of people came, ranging from freshmen to graduate students and faculty. Many of them had found themselves dissatisfied with recent linguistic philosophy, and yet knew that in some way language has deeply mattered to philosophy. I tried to describe, in a few case studies, some remarkable ways in which language has mattered, and then speculated on why this should have been so. The approach was often more historical than the audience expected, but to understand why language mattered we had to think not only how it has mattered but also when it has mattered. None of us was concerned with boring and ephemeral questions such as whether linguistic analysis is worthy or iniquitous. We were trying to understand the structure of something very striking about philosophical speculation. I hope that students elsewhere with doubts and fascinations similar to ours may find this book helpful.

1. Strategy

I shall not begin by saying why language matters to philosophy, but start with some evidence, examining a few familiar problems in metaphysics and epistemology that have been influenced by theories about language. The main body of the book will illustrate how language has, from time to time, mattered to philosophers. It is a collection of case studies, which can usefully introduce newcomers to the subject. Only the final chapter tries to guess about the nature of language and philosophy in an attempt to explain some features of the case studies. Only then do I try to answer the question Why does language matter? The final conjectures, although by no means original, are at present non-standard. The reader is not obliged to accept them. In the case studies I aim at objectivity, providing data on the basis of which you can judge the situation for yourself. This objectivity is slightly spurious because I inevitably select and interpret the data in my own way. I try to refrain from editorializing until the end.

Before getting down to work, a variety of remarks are needed, mostly negative. First, many philosophers writing in English seem to have settled down to discuss the *pure* theory of meaning. They do not appear to study language and meaning in order to understand some philosophical problem – what we could call *applied* philosophy of language – but write almost exclusively about the nature of meaning itself. A sizeable proportion of potential philosophy graduate students applying to English-speaking universities say they want to do research in the theory of meaning. So in the short run we may expect articles about the pure theory of meaning to form an increasingly large part of many philosophical journals, dissertations, and university examination papers. But if we look at older works in the same 'empiricist' tradition as ours – Hobbes, Locke, Berkeley, Hume, or Mill, say – we find that discussions of language are almost always directed towards central non-linguistic issues in philosophy. Equally, G. E. Moore, Ludwig Wittgenstein, and J. L. Austin, so often regarded as the founding fathers of philosophy of language, were all preoccupied with traditional problems: Moore, for example, with ethics, perception, and knowledge of the external world, or Wittgenstein, in his *Philosophical Investigations*, with the nature of the human mind. It is notable that Noam Chomsky, by trade a linguist, has also urged striking views about the nature of mind on the basis of his work on grammar. The Olympian figures of our time do not in this respect differ from their predecessors. Theories about language enter the most memorable philosophy in order to be applied to central philosophical issues. So my contrast between 'pure' and 'applied' theory is not between the most significant contributions of now and of the past, but rather between present hack work and that of previous generations. Only recently have day-to-day routine teaching and writing in philosophy become embroiled in theories of meaning for their own sake. This book will be more like older hack work: the case studies will mostly be theories about applications, rather than philosophizing about language for its own sake.

This introduces a prejudice, and loads the scales against some possible answers to my question. You might expect a book with my title to explain why meaning matters to philosophy, whereas I shall sometimes argue, paradoxically, that the pure theory of meaning does not matter much to philosophy, although language does. The situation may prove to resemble that of philosophical psychology. Psychology was once part of philosophy and now is one or several independent disciplines. The stimulus–response model of behaviour comes out of the empiricist philosophy, and quite specific models – like the association theory of learning that has by now acquired a fully mathematized format – go back through a chain of philosophers: to James Mill, to David Hartley, to David Hume (who called the theory of association his most novel contribution). Thus what was once deemed a central topic for philosophers became a separate study with its own canons of investigation and its own standards of excellence. This does not mean it is of no interest to philosophers, for the philosophical mind turns to any discipline where there is conceptual difficulty. Philosophical groping about in experimental psychology is, however, no more central to philosophy than philosophical speculation about quantum mechanics (part of what would once have been called natural philosophy) or statistical inference (part of what would once have been called logic).

Some philosophy of language can likewise be expected to hive off its own new sciences. But despite the fact that there is an autonomous academic discipline called experimental psychology, there remains a residual subject called philosophy of mind, arguably the most recalcitrant of topics with which philosophers now engage. The parallel that I foresee is this. Much of the pure theory of meaning that preoccupies our generation of philosophers will very quickly become autonomous, but a body of essentially philosophical questions about language will persist.

A fine example of this trend is furnished by the theory of 'presupposition' advanced by P. T. Geach and P. F. Strawson about 1950, by way of criticism of a theory propounded by Bertrand Russell in 1905. Both writers, but especially Strawson, held that presupposition was an important concept for understanding the nature of meaning. This had a good run in the philosophical arena, but within twenty years had been picked up by the linguists, and in 1970 became almost a steady diet for papers and seminars in some schools of linguistics. I do not know if this was a passing fad, or will prove a permanent part of any future linguistic theory. Here we have an idea, first promulgated by Russell in a theory of meaning that had immediate metaphysical applications, then transformed into philosophers' pure theory for its own sake, and finally lifted wholesale into linguistics, which may be its proper site. Yet although some applied theory of meaning thus becomes first 'pure' and then autonomous linguistics, some leftover philosophical problems about language will perhaps prove as intractable as problems in the residual philosophy of mind.

At the end of the book I shall try to say why there will be a philosophical labyrinth with language at its centre, but before doing the case studies, I should put aside some quite unimportant ways in which language has mattered to philosophy. To call them unimportant is once again to prejudice the outcome. Some philosophers would say that these unimportant ways are precisely why language is so crucial to philosophy. The vindication of my prejudice can only come later, by displaying something more important than the following elementary ways in which language has affected our discipline.

As a matter of course, language matters to philosophy in the way it matters to all extended thought: we express and communicate our ideas in language. But why should the study of language matter more to philosophy than to, say, zoology? There is one answer to this question which is correct but which is not the important answer. It lies in the fact that philosophy has to do with a special kind of perplexity where we hardly know what questions to pose. The problem of free will is readily felt by many people in many walks of life. Indeed, although most of our problems arise in the historical context of Western culture, the malaise about free will is more widespread. The problem is not open to any 'scientific' enquiry thus far imagined, and many will argue that it could not be. Some thinkers attack the problem of free will by distinguishing different notions of freedom or meanings of the word 'free'. In one sense we are free – free enough for concepts of morality and responsibility to come into play. In another sense we are not free, and all that happens now is determined by what has happened earlier. According to this 'soft determinism', as William James called it, determinism is supposed to express a true doctrine in one sense of the words, and a false doctrine in another. Plenty of philosophers have argued that the problem about free will arises from what Hobbes called the 'inconstancy' of language. The same word, they say, is inconstant – it can have several meanings. Even philosophers who argue for a simple determinism have to show that in their arguments the word 'free' is used with a constant sense, leading up to the conclusion that we are not free.

Thus one reason why language matters to philosophy and not to zoology is that philosophers are often concerned with domains where our common ways of thinking and arguing lead us not to clarity and a satisfactory technical language, but rather to ambiguity, equivocation, contradiction, and paradox. A plausible way to attack the difficulty is to try to trace the paradoxes to confusions between different concepts. The symptom is confusion between different senses of words. In particular, if you think that some earlier philosopher has got things wrong, you may say with Francis Bacon, in *The Advancement of Learning*, that,

Although we think we govern our words, . . . certain it is that words, as a Tartar's bow, do shoot back upon the understanding of the wisest, and mightily entangle and pervert the judgment. So that it is almost necessary, in all controversies and disputations, to imitate the wisdom of the mathematicians, in setting down in the very beginning the definitions of our words and terms, that others may know how we accept and understand them, and whether they concur with us or no. For it cometh to pass, for want of this, that we are sure to end there where we ought to have begun, which is – in questions and differences about words.

This pleasing aphorism is echoed in many another writer. Careful attention to words is an important feature of philosophical debate, and definition can help avoid equivocation. This is an unimportant way in which language matters to philosophy. We do indeed have a danger, graver than in other disciplines, of entanglement, 'perversion', and empty speech. This trifling feature of language and philosophy will not dominate our case studies.

There is a second minor way in which language has mattered to philosophy, and which seems almost the opposite of what I have just described. It arises from the belief that we shall avoid confusion if only we attend closely enough to distinctions actually present in common speech. So on the one hand language has been held to matter to philosophy because common speech leads us into confusion; the solution, often urged, is to produce exact definitions. But now we have the opposite opinion: reflective use of common speech is the very way to avoid confusion, and defining new terms will actually augment confusion.

This second opinion is often thought to be a new thing, epitomized by Wittgenstein's opinion that 'ordinary language is all right'. The only thing new is the widespread use of techniques of linguistic analysis. For example, Locke's Cartesian predecessors had much debated questions about the essence of matter, Descartes himself contending that its essence lies in extension, taking up space. Incidental to this debate is the question of how *matter* and *bodies* are related. Locke thought that he had a short proof that matter and body are not identical:

if the ideas these two terms ['matter' and 'body'] stood for were precisely the same, they might indifferently in all places be put for one another. But we see that though it be proper to say, There is one matter of all bodies, one cannot say, There is one body of all matters: we familiarly say one body is bigger than another; but it sounds harsh (and I think is never used) to say one matter is bigger than another.[1]

Locke claims that we can learn something relevant to a deep

1. *An Essay Concerning Human Understanding*, iii.x.15.

philosophical debate by considering the nuances of seven-teenth-century English, of what 'sounds harsh', and of what it is 'proper to say'.

Nor is this technique restricted to negative conclusions. Thus Spinoza, in the course of evolving a remarkable theory of truth, begins by telling us that we cannot hope to get the matter right unless we start to examine how the word 'true' is used in common speech:

Since common use first discovered these words ['true' and 'false'] which were only afterwards used by the philosophers, it seems pertinent for anyone who inquires into the first meaning of a word to see what it first denoted in common use, especially in the absence of other causes which might be drawn from the nature of language for the purposes of the investigation. The first meaning of true and false seems to have had its origin in narratives; a narrative was called true when it related a fact which had really occurred, and false when it related a fact which had nowhere occurred.[2]

To conclude: there are two well-known minor ways in which language has mattered to philosophy. On the one hand there is a belief that if only we produce good definitions, often marking out different senses of words that are confused in common speech, we will avoid the conceptual traps that ensnared our forefathers. On the other hand is a belief that if only we attend sufficiently closely to our mother tongue and make explicit the distinctions there implicit, we shall avoid the conceptual traps. One or the other of these curiously con-trary beliefs may nowadays be most often thought of as an answer to the question Why does language matter to philoso-phy? Neither seems to me enough.

I have now avowed two prejudices: I opt for applied theory of meaning rather than pure theory of meaning, and I hold that no kind of conceptual minesweeping – neither Bacon's definitions to avoid the errors of the 'vulgar', nor

2. *Thoughts on Metaphysics*, I., vi.3; trans. by F. A. Hayes in *Spin-oza, Earlier Philosophical Writings* (Indianapolis, Ind.: Bobbs-Merrill), p. 122.

Locke's attention to what in vulgar speech it is 'proper to say' – is the central reason why language matters to philosophy. My case studies will be severely constrained by these prejudices. There are other constraints. First, the case studies should be relatively easy. By 'easy' I mean fairly easy for many of us, here, now, to get our minds around. As an example of something that is not easy, one may take those discussions that fall loosely under the heading 'private language argument', and which derive from Wittgenstein. These are among the more profound speculations of modern times. They have deep implications for the philosophy of mind. They are much too difficult for any case study. I do not understand the ramifications of the argument and it is clear that various commentators take the argument in different, incompatible, senses.

As an example of something that is easy, take Norman Malcolm's little book called *Dreaming*. Descartes crystallized an old question, 'How do I know I am not dreaming right now?' Malcolm proposed a completely novel answer which is, aside from matters of fine detail, quite intelligible to most of us. I shall use it in Chapter 10. We may think it a fine analysis or a ghastly absurdity or something in between, but at least we can understand what the argument is. I do not mean that it is easy for us to reach agreement on whether the argument is valid, but only that there is no problem about what is being argued, and how it is being argued. One critic has said of a recent collection of papers about Wittgenstein's private language argument, that the accounts in that anthology are so disparate that subsequent scholars would have to imagine that the authors worked from different texts of Wittgenstein, or that there were several Wittgensteins.[3] No such problem arises for most of my cases under study.

3. C. W. K. Mundle, *Critique of Linguistic Philosophy* (Oxford: University Press, 1969), p. 4, referring to G. Pitcher's anthology, *Wittgenstein, The Philosophical Investigations: A Collection of Critical Essays* (New York: Anchor, 1966).

There are, however, many reasons why I cannot be entirely faithful to the intention to have 'easy' case studies. For example, we ought to have some contemporary work before us, for fear that our conjectures have not already been bypassed or falsified. This entails chapters on material that has not yet entirely crystallized. I shall take two very different metaphysicians who have had much impact on recent philosophy of language: Donald Davidson and Paul Feyerabend. Neither has yet given us a definitive book. They present an ample collection of interrelated doctrines in scattered essays. Each has an important group of disciples. Since the work of each man is complicated and not yet fully nor even consistently articulated, it is not easy. We must take it up because the speculations at the end of the book would be worthless if they were made in ignorance of the present.

The work of Davidson and Feyerabend is hard to obtain: it lies in many journals and volumes, some obscure. This already provides a reason for trying to summarize *their* work, rather than choosing more familiar figures of the immediate past. Some readers will be surprised to find hardly a reference to the late J. L. Austin. The two philosophers of language now living who have exercised the greatest influence on Anglo-Americans are surely P. F. Strawson and W. v. O. Quine. In attempting to assess certain elements in the contemporary scene, I shall say relatively little about them. This is partly because each has already given us at least one classic, epitomizing much of his system of thought. We possess Strawson's *Individuals* and Quine's *Word and Object;* moreover the philosophical magazines are full of excellent argument, pro and con, concerning these great systems of our time. The situation with Austin is less satisfactory, for he died in full vigour, but we do at least have the totality of his incompleted work, and the interested reader can easily follow this for himself. Moreover, I shall not say much about the body of work sometimes called 'Oxford linguistic philosophy'. One can learn a good deal about its practitioners, and how they and their opponents conceive of themselves, in several excellent anthologies listed in the bibliography at the back of this book.

In trying to say something about contemporary matters I shall severely restrict myself in one respect. I shall gratify the requirement of 'ease' for the present audience by examining only work in the Anglo-American traditions. So I shall seem to be tackling the question 'Why does language matter to philosophers who write, or have come to write, chiefly in English?' Yet I shall be trying to answer a much more general question which, for convenience, is illustrated by English case studies. I should be delighted to top up with the work of Gilles Deleuze, Jacques Derrida, Michel Foucault, or other prominent contemporary French figures, and indeed their cases might provide better evidence for the conjectures of my concluding chapter than the material presented here. It would also be very helpful to study the linguistic turn in contemporary German Marxism. I regretfully leave all these aside because it would be unprofitable to provide enough background to understand the various idioms which are so relatively alien to most of us. It is a manifest fact that immense consciousness of language is at the present time characteristic of every main stream in Western philosophy. We are, ultimately, not concerned with why language mattered to some people in Oxford in the 1950s or to other people in Cambridge, Massachusetts in the 1960s or to yet others in Paris after 1968. We are interested in why language matters to (Western) philosophy.

Clearly, then, we wish to examine what is happening now. But we require historical perspective because it is important to know when language has mattered to philosophy. As far as the quest for definitions or the attempt to avoid conceptual confusion go, the answer is surely 'always'. Plato's *Euthyphro* is explicitly a quest for a definition to end confusion. But if there are other, deeper, reasons why language matters to philosophy, it is not a foregone conclusion that they have always been major reasons. Indeed there may be transformations in our ways of conceiving ourselves and the world which make language matter to philosophy now in a way that is entirely novel.

It is seldom easy to grasp old philosophical debates. I shall do the best I can for the present readership chiefly by choosing empiricist philosophers writing in English. They are most familiar and we avoid the difficulties of translation. Thus in speaking of the past I am using the same principles of selection as when dealing with the immediate present. I do not believe that the outcome is unduly influenced by this decision. I could, for example, choose specific treatments by Spinoza and reconstruct a theory of language essential to these. But the texts are not well known and those who are familiar with them would query some of my textual analyses.

There is one way in which my national principle of historical selection is manifestly defective, for it excludes any work by Kant or Hegel. They may be hard to understand, their idiom may be alien, but the transformations on the Western view of the world which they expressed and to which they gave added impetus are fundamental. Someone else will be able to write more deeply on my question, why does language matter, taking case studies drawn solely from the corpus of Kantians and Hegelians. No matter: with any luck, that author will reach about the same conclusions as I do.

British empiricists are used because they are familiar and easy. Unfortunately I shall sometimes have to show that even they are unfamiliar and hard. To begin to work on them one must take some stand on that antique term of art, 'idea', which occurs on almost the first page of nearly every major figure, and dominates the whole discussion. Although this leads to difficult terrain, the very difficulty can be put to some use. At the end of the book we shall be chiefly concerned with the way in which language has come to serve as the interface between, on the one side, the way in which we conceive the world and, on the other, something dimly reminiscent of the Cartesian 'ego', the knowing self. In the seventeenth century the doctrine of what philosophers then called ideas provided a parallel interface, between what they conceived of as the world and their Cartesian egos. One transformation that we have to note and to explain is how the doctrine of ideas, taken literally, could once seem so inevitable, now seems so strange, and yet manifestly treats many of our problems in what many commentators deem to be something like our ways.

A. The heyday of ideas

2. Thomas Hobbes' mental discourse

Locke and other empiricists have much to say about language but it is not until the time of J. S. Mill's *System of Logic* (1844) that one regularly began a philosophy book like this: 'Book I, *Of Names and Propositions*; Chapter 1: *Of the Necessity of commencing with an Analysis of Language*'. Mill deems an analysis of language necessary for the minor reasons I stated in Chapter 1. 'An inquiry into language . . . is needful to guard against the errors to which it gives rise.' 'But there is,' he continues, 'another reason, of a still more fundamental nature' for asking about language, namely that without such an enquiry, the logician cannot examine what Mill rather solemnly calls the *import of Propositions*. The whole work, like that of many a predecessor, is divided into four parts, of which the first is about language. The predecessors, however, do not usually say, in their titles, that they are treating of language. On the contrary, the titles are about *ideas*. A recent behaviourist trend may tempt us to read such students of 'ideas' as discussing meaning and language acquisition, but they did not see things quite our way. They did think language matters to philosophy, but to understand how it mattered to them one must try to take them on their own terms.

First, what is the point of language? In 1651 Hobbes wrote, 'the general use of speech, is to transfer our mental discourse, into verbal; or the train of our thoughts into a train of words' (*Leviathan*, I.4). He certainly had a plausible theory. In each of us there is a chain of thoughts. That is pre-linguistic, but it is handy to be able to express it in words. It is hard to remember complex ratiocination without verbaliz-ing it, and it is not possible to convey difficult thoughts or reasonings to others without language. We may agree with Berkeley's shrewd counter-observation, some sixty years later, that 'the communicating of ideas marked by words is not the chief and only end of language, as is commonly supposed. There are other ends, as the raising of some passion, the exciting to or deterring from an action, the putting the mind in some particular disposition.'[1] That shows only that com-munication of thoughts is not the *sole* end of language, and Berkeley himself has an eloquent evocation of the Hobbesian picture when he speaks of speech raising in your breast the thoughts already present in mine.

Hobbes' phrase 'mental discourse' is instructive. There is something mental, enough like language to call it discourse, but which is logically prior to language. Seventeenth-century manuals very often recommend that we should strip our thought of as much language as possible, because public lan-guage, unlike mental discourse, is so prone to abuse. If only we could manage to get down to the ideas about which we are thinking – or simply think in ideas – then, they say, we should be less likely to fall into error.

If we are to make any sense at all out of theories of lan-guage of this period, we must acknowledge that at the time one accepted the priority of mental discourse to public speech. I emphasize this because although it is such a natural theory to hold, recent philosophy has done much to discour-age the picture of inner discourse to which outer discourse is subservient. Remember we are not at present seeking a 'true' theory, but trying to understand how theories about language matter to philosophy. In the next four chapters I shall exam-ine some doctrines dominant from the birth of Hobbes

1. Introduction to *The Principles of Human Knowledge*, sec. 20.

(1588) to the death of Berkeley (1753); or, to narrow the scope, from Hobbes' *Leviathan* (1651) to Berkeley's *Principles* (1710). Berkeley explicitly argues that as soon as we abandon certain errors about language, we will conclude that to be is to be perceived. 'Philosophical idealism' is the doctrine that there is no matter, and that all existents are mental. Berkeley, the chief philosophical idealist of all time, deliberately contends that as soon as you correctly understand the nature of language you will become an idealist. Staggering implications are thus alleged to follow from his opinions about language. There is no point in trying to get his idealism by his argument merely by translating it into our late-twentieth-century opinions on language. That leads only to nonsense. One must make the imaginative leap of believing in, among other things, mental discourse. It does not require that much imagination because for most of us it was our native untutored theory of language.

The difference between that time and ours can perhaps best be illustrated by transforming Wittgenstein's dictum that 'all the sentences of our everyday language, just as they stand, are in perfect logical order' (*Tractatus* 5.5563). Three centuries ago the dictum would have been: Our ideas are all right as they stand (although some are perceived more clearly than others). Trouble comes only when you replace the train of thoughts by the train of words, when (in Bacon's aphorism) the words 'shoot back upon the understanding of the wisest, and mightily entangle and pervert the judgment'.

There is a problem if you think mental discourse is all right but verbal discourse leads to error, for we cannot communicate except verbally. Our philosophers did not shirk the conclusion: verbal discourse is appropriate for communication, but for real thinking, they said, try to get as far as you can from words. Descartes' *Rules for the Direction of the Mind* are famous because of their author, but are entirely typical of the manuals in circulation at the time. The gist of the advice is that to avoid error we must train ourselves to 'scrutinize' our ideas 'with steadfast mental gaze'.[2] Stop speaking and start looking, looking inside yourself. What is one to look *at*? The answer is given by that code word 'idea'. I shall postpone an enquiry into what our philosophers thought ideas are. First let us become aware of the extreme difficulty of pinning a 'theory of meaning' on any philosopher of those times. I shall work around Hobbes, partly because he was the last great philosopher of the time not to succumb to using 'ideas' as a panacea for many problems of language, the world, and the mind.

We can begin to understand the difficulty of attaching a theory of meaning to a philosopher by taking the case of Hobbes, and put off until the next chapter the difficulties occasioned by former uses of the word 'idea'. Consider what Hobbes says a name is:

Words so connected as that they become signs of our thoughts, are called SPEECH, of which every part is a *name*. But seeing (as is said) both marks and signs are necessary for the acquiring of philosophy, (marks by which we may remember our own thoughts, and signs by which we may make our thoughts known to others), names do both these offices; but they serve for marks before they be used as signs . . . So that the nature of a name consists principally in this, that it is a mark taken for memory's sake; but it serves also by accident to signify and make known to others what we remember ourselves. (*Elements of Philosophy: Concerning Body,* i.ii.3)

What theory is this? We can usefully employ a classification due to William Alston, who distinguishes three theories of meaning: ideational, referential, and behavioural.[3] I shall not define the term 'theory of meaning' until Chapter 5: let us learn first by example, wading directly into Alston's categories. They provide excellent labels. If in the end I am

2. *Rules for the Direction of the Mind,* XII, trans. E. S. Haldane and G. R. T. Ross, in *The Philosophical Works of Descartes* (Cambridge: University Press, 1911), I, p. 46.
3. *The Philosophy of Language* (Englewood Cliffs, N.J.: Prentice-Hall, 1964), Ch. 1.

unhappy to apply them, especially to Hobbes or Berkeley, I have been glad of such tags to illustrate the difficulty of applying any tags at all.

Alston's classification works roughly as follows. An *ideational* theory holds that the meaning of a word (e.g. of those words that Hobbes would have called names) is the idea in our mind for which it stands. Thus if I say, 'I went to Penny's barbecue party last night', I have an idea of a particular outdoor event, namely Penny's barbecue, and that idea is what I mean by the phrase 'Penny's barbecue'. The *referential* theory, on the other hand, says that the meaning of 'Penny's barbecue' is the actual event, namely Penny's barbecue, to which I refer – or, if that event did not take place, the referentialist produces a theory showing how the phrase 'Penny's barbecue' gets its meaning from items to which I can correctly refer, such as, presumably, Penny and her penchant for outdoor festivity. The way in which Bertrand Russell made such a theory work is the topic of Chapter 7. Finally *behavioural* theories analyse meaning in terms of what people do on hearing words, and perhaps what speakers intend hearers to do. Alston treats these three kinds of theory as if they are mutually exclusive and incompatible.

Locke, who wrote about forty years after Hobbes, is often offered as a prime example of an ideationist. He certainly says, 'The use, then, of words, is to be sensible marks of ideas; and the ideas they stand for are their proper and imdiate signification' (*Essay*, III.ii.1). Indeed, says Locke, no one can apply words 'as marks, immediately, to anything else but the ideas that he himself hath' (III.ii.2) In short *'words* ... came to be made use of by men as the signs of their ideas' (III.ii.1).

Locke, you may think, is pigeon-holed, for what can be meant by 'proper and immediate signification' but 'meaning'? If a word is a sign of an idea, then surely we rightly paraphrase this by saying the word means the idea? We cannot answer such questions with certainty until we know what ideas are, but as a beginning, we can ask about signs. Hobbes tells us that the use of words is as marks or signs. 'Names ordered in speech' are 'signs of conceptions', not of things in themselves. So it looks as if Hobbes is going to fall into the ideationist category, for the conceptions are surely part of the mental discourse, and that, presumably, is what is 'meant'. Unfortunately, our classification does not go so easily. Here is a crucial paragraph by Hobbes:

> those things we call SIGNS are the *antecedents of their conse-quents, and the consequents of their antecedents, as often as we observe them to go before or follow after in the same manner.* For example, a thick cloud is a sign of rain to follow, and rain a sign that a cloud has gone before, for this reason only, that we seldom see clouds without the consequence of rain, nor rain at any time but when a cloud has gone before. And of signs, some are *natural,* whereof I have already given an example, others are *arbitrary,* namely, those we make choice of at our own pleasure, as a bush hung up, signifies that wine is to be sold there; a stone set in the ground signifies the bound of a field; and words so and so connected, signify the cogitations and motions of our mind. (*Elements* II.ii.2)

Once we attend carefully to this definition of 'sign' it becomes very difficult to foist any theory of meaning on to Hobbes. *A* signifies *B* when *A* regularly follows or precedes *B*. In Hobbes' opinion, words regularly follow or precede thoughts. I hear the expression 'Penny's barbecue' and thereupon think of broiled mutton or pork. I infer, from your uttering the words, that your thoughts are similar. Or, thinking about the barbecue I am led to utter words from which you infer *my* chain of thought. In this way words signify – are signs of – thoughts. Hobbes says that words signify thoughts. Does it follow that in his sense they 'mean' thoughts?

Hobbes is supposed to have an ideational theory of meaning. That (according to Alston) would be inconsistent with his having a referential theory of meaning. Yet Hobbes may perfectly well agree to the two following propositions. First, words signify thoughts and ideas, that is, words are regularly uttered after thoughts occur, and thereby signify them, and thoughts regulary occur after words are uttered, again showing that words are signs of thoughts. Secondly, and consistent with this, what words mean is the things they are about. For example, a suitable utterance of the phrase 'Penny's barbecue' produces in me the thought of Penny's barbecue, which shows the words signify the thought. But what the words actually mean could still be what they refer to, namely, a particular outdoor party, Penny's barbecue. In short, although an ideational theory of meaning is customarily pinned on Hobbes, what he actually says is entirely consistent with a referential theory of meaning.

Not only is a referential theory consistent with what Hobbes says, but some of his texts could be used to foist one on him. He asserts that 'things named, are either the *objects* themselves; or the *conception* itself that we have of man, as shape and motion' (*Human Nature,* v.3). So although all words are signs of ideas, they may name either objects, as a particular man, or certain general conceptions, such as shape. The meanings of words are, it might be contended, the individual objects or the abstract notions which the words denote.

Must we now conclude that Hobbes is a referentialist and not an ideationist after all? Not at all. Consider this possibly anomalous passage:

that the sound of this word *stone* should be the sign of a stone, cannot be understood in any sense but this, that he that hears it collects that he that pronounces it thinks of a stone. (*Elements* I.ii.5)

One can string this thought out with other quotations to get something markedly like the recently canvassed *intentional* theory of meaning advocated by H. P. Grice.[4] Here is an up-to-date behavioural theory. Grice, like Hobbes, distinguishes between natural and arbitrary signs ('natural' and 'non-natu-

---

4. 'Meaning', *The Philosophical Review,* LXVI (1957), 377-88; 'Utterer's Meaning and Intensions', *Ibid.* LXXVIII (1969), 147-77.

ral' meaning in Grice) and proceeds to analyse non-natural meaning in terms of what the speaker intends the hearer to 'collect' from what is pronounced. Thus, in this most subtle and sensible of behavioural theories, Grice does not attend to such static features as the reference of the words, or the ideas in the mind, but rather to a mode of behaviour, namely communication and intention to communicate. Some readers may guess that Hobbes' analysis of signification in terms of what the hearer can collect from the speaker's words, is a shift to a communication-oriented behavioural theory of meaning.

Although referential, behavioural, and ideational theories of meaning are supposed to be mutually exclusive, Hobbes may have held or toyed with all three. That is one possibility. Another is that these categories, apt for much modern work, are not the right categories for analysing Hobbes. Indeed, although Hobbes plainly thought language mattered to philosophy, it is possible that he did not have a theory of meaning at all. That would certainly explain why his words do not readily slot into Alston's categories: he was not in the same line of business.

Hobbes did have some theories about thinking. Nowadays we increasingly link thought and language. Hobbes and his peers made thought a matter of mental discourse, conceptions, or ideas. Mental discourse, albeit aided by public language, was supposed to be autonomous. Modern philosophers disagree with that. Is this because, if we are right about language now, we have learned to correct Hobbes' errors? Perhaps. But it is also possible that today we are talking about something different. Perhaps language, as we now conceive it, is not a topic that people could have contemplated earlier. Perhaps it is a topic treating of a new phenomenon. Perhaps the relations between knowledge, thought, and language in our time are not the same as they used to be. At any rate we have now acquired a radically different philosophy of language. Our authors tend to dismiss Hobbes' outlook in terms such as these:

The second weakness in this account was the presumed interme-
diary of phantasms between things and names which was part
and parcel of *his peculiarly private theory of meaning*. It derived
from his general view that we are confronted with our own phantasms of things, not with things themselves, and from his
mechanical theory. He thought that our conceptions are marked
by names which are like signposts rearing themselves out of an
unfamiliar country; these marks, when uttered as words, bring to
the minds of those who hear them similar conceptions as they,
too, go on their journeys. But this presupposes not only that the
speaker and the hearer always have a similar conception when
they hear a word, but also that they always have *some* conception. And by 'conception' Hobbes meant a concrete determinate
image. Both these assumptions seem plainly false.[5]

There is a possibility that Peters did not envisage: Hobbes
did have a theory of signification, that is, of the sign relation,
but this sign relation has to do with immediate precedence
and consequence. There is little evidence that Hobbes held an
ideational, or a referential, or a behavioural theory of meaning. Each of the three, though supposed to be incompatible
with the other two, is perfectly compatible with what Hobbes
says. I suspect that he did not have a 'peculiarly private
theory of meaning', *because he did not have a theory of
meaning.*

It remains true that Hobbes did believe that words are like
'signposts rearing themselves out of an unfamiliar country'
(as Peters puts it). At any rate they bring to mind thoughts,
and thoughts also lead to the production of words. There is an
obvious objection to this doctrine which Peters has in mind in
the passage quoted. There is in general nothing, it is argued,
for which words are signs in Hobbes' sense. That is where
ideas come in. They are supposed to be that for which our
words are signs. It has recently been emphasized among
working philosophers that in general there need be no particular idea, in *our* sense of the word 'idea', in my mind when

5. Richard Peters, *Hobbes* (Harmondsworth: Penguin, 1956), pp.
134-5, first italics added.

(to use an example of Wittgenstein) I shout *'March!'* Doubtless when I shout that word in reply to the query, 'When is your birthday?' no particular end-of-winter thought need have passed through my mind to give a correct answer; equally when I utter the same word, in the same tone, to a gang of prisoners I may be mindlessly dreaming of dahlias and still get the men to march in exactly the way I intended. Clearly in these two circumstances the word 'march' has quite different meanings, and its utterance produces quite different kinds of effects, but there need not be anything particular going on in my mind for me to achieve these effects. There need not have been before me, in the one case, a month-idea, and in the other, a foot-slogging-idea. In both cases the only images before my mind at the time of utterance may have been flowers.

These reflections do not prove, in any direct way, that there may not have been an idea, in some *other* sense of the word 'idea', for which the word 'march' was, on one or the other occasion, a sign. To explore that possibility we must understand that difficult seventeenth-century word 'idea'. It will be hard, but we shall try to do so in the next chapter, because in the end it will help tell us why language matters to philosophy now.

At a more modest level it is easy to see that Hobbes did think that language does matter to philosophy. He is, of course, most remembered for his theory of the state, and is usually taken as the standard example of a view that emerged in his lifetime. Individuals, whose life, he said, is 'nasty, brutish and short', must contract into or submit to a state with sovereign powers. This is necessary to make life even tolerable, let alone bounteous. His work on language is not peripheral to his 'republic'. On the contrary, his chief works on political theory, such as *Leviathan*, all begin with a study of human nature and man's communication. The political animal is necessarily a speaking animal, and to understand politics, thought Hobbes, one needs a good theory of speech.

This may seem at odds with my contention that no particular theory of public meaning or communication can be pinned on Hobbes, but it is not. The public discourse of politics is, in his opinion, entirely parasitic upon mental discourse. Indeed it is instructive to compare the thrust of his theories of the state and of speech. In the case of the state, individuals are constituted prior to a state that makes sense and exacts obligations only in terms of the needs of individuals and the contracts into which they enter. Likewise, Hobbesian mental discourse is constituted prior to the public discourse that is derived from it. Modern empiricist philosophy has turfed out the latter doctrine, but is still, in such works as John Rawls' *A Theory of Justice*, wedded to the former.

3. Port Royal's ideas

The most influential logic book after Aristotle and before the end of the nineteenth century is *Logic, or the Art of Thinking*. It was written mostly by Antoine Arnauld and Pierre Nicole, and was published in Paris in 1662. Both men were associated with the Jansenist sect, a protesting and largely intellectual group that remained within the Catholic Church, although not without the occasional papal denunciation. Their retreat was a French monastery at Port Royal, and they published anonymously, so this book is commonly called the Port Royal *Logic*. Although it professes to be a few easy lessons by which a tutor may instruct a young gentleman, the work went through an enormous number of editions, and was the prescribed logic text at Oxford and Edinburgh quite late in the nineteenth century. Its influence is comparable to that of its sister volume, the 1660 Port Royal *Grammar*, which, as we shall see in Chapter 6, has been taken, by Noam Chomsky, as the very model of profound linguistic enquiry.

The format of many a commonplace philosophical treatise at least until the time of J. S. Mill is a book in four parts, patterned after the *Logic*. Immediate satellites of the work were Malebranche and Locke, and one occasionally needs the book to understand Berkeley too. Just like the *Logic*, Berkeley begins his introduction to his *Principles* by telling us that he is going to discuss language, but immediately takes up the topic of ideas. The two are intimately connected in his mind, but what is an idea? English commentators, correctly noting the ample references to Locke, consult that philosopher to see what Berkeley could have meant. They are immediately beset by distaste. Geoffrey Warnock, for example, raises eyebrows of despair:

On this central point it is impossible to elicit from Locke a clear answer. By the term 'idea' he confessedly means almost anything one cares to choose; he says that term stands for 'whatsoever is the object of the understanding when a man thinks'; that it means the same as 'phantasm, notion, species'; and also that it stands for objects of perception generally.[1]

Similarly David Armstrong introducing a Berkeley anthology tells us that:

Locke uses the word 'idea in an extraordinarily wide way. It covers *at least*:
(a) sense-perceptions (sense impressions);
(b) bodily sensations (such things as pains or tickles);
(c) mental images;
(d) thoughts and concepts.
The use of one word to cover this heterogeneous class of things leads Locke into all sorts of errors.[2]

I am reminded of the preface to Michel Foucault's *The Order of Things*, which recalls a story by Georges Borges (the Argentinian poet and fantasist whose favourite philosopher is, as it happens, Berkeley). Apparently Borges pretends to quote

a 'certain Chinese encyclopaedia' in which it is written that 'animals are divided into: (a) belonging to the Emperor, (b) embalmed, (c) tame, (d) sucking pigs, (e) sirens, (f) fabulous, (g) stray dogs, (h) included in the present classification, (i) frenzied, (j) innumerable, (k) drawn with a very fine camelhair brush, (l) *et cetera*, (m) having just broken the water pitcher, (n) that from a long way off look like flies'.

Foucault concludes his paragraph by speaking of the 'stark

1. *Berkeley* (Harmondsworth: Penguin, 1953), p. 64.
2. *Berkeley's Philosophical Writings* (New York: Collier; London: Collier–Macmillan, 1965), p. 8.

impossibility of thinking *that*'. Clearly Warnock and Armstrong have the same experiences on contemplating the ideas of Locke and Berkeley that we have in this fabulous classification of Chinese animals: the stark impossibility of that heterogeneous class 'idea'.

Now contrast the first chapter of *The Art of Thinking*: '*Some words are so clear that they cannot be explained by others, for none are more clear and more simple. "Idea" is such a word.*'[3] Nothing is more clear than 'idea'!

Ideas, for these authors, form no artificial class of disparate entities; *idea* is the most elemental kind of entity imaginable, beyond possibility of definition. At most one needs (apparently) the warning that to conceive an idea 'does not signify, exclusively, to imagine an idea'. I cannot form an image of a figure with exactly one thousand sides but I can reason accurately about chiliahedra, and this involves conceiving the idea. Likewise, says the *Logic*, we have ideas of God and of free will but can form no image of either.

But why should images and the objects of reasoning be put in the same class at all? It is not only modern commentators who are puzzled. Kant was visibly angry. The word 'idea', far from being a word of ordinary language conscripted by philosophers, was introduced into various vernaculars in order to translate one of Plato's terms of art. Kant restores the word 'idea' to what he takes to be Plato's sense, and says, 'anyone who has familiarised himself with these distinctions must find it intolerable to hear the representation of the colour, red, called an idea' (*Critique of Pure Reason* A 320/B 377). Why is what is so starkly impossible for us and intolerable to Kant a paradigm of clarity and simplicity for the British disciples of the Port Royal *Logic*?

The answer must lie in the first sentence of Part I of that book: 'We have no knowledge of what is *outside* us except by

---

3. Antoine Arnauld, *The Art of Thinking*, trans. James Dickoff and Patricia James (Indianapolis, Ind.: Bobbs–Merrill, 1964), p. 31.

the mediation of the ideas *within* us.' The Cartesian *ego* has set the stage. The *ego* able to contemplate what is within it ponders what lies outside. There are some objects that we can contemplate without being logically committed to the existence of anything other than the ego. These objects are ideas. Nowadays we hear the brusque retort that there need be no single kind of object available for contemplation in this way, but that is to argue in reverse. What makes for a 'kind' of object but some basic principle of classification? The principle of classification is clear: an idea is any object that can be contemplated by a thinking being without existential commitment to anything except that being.

'Existential commitment' is best explained by example. If someone asks me over the telephone what I am doing at the moment, I may reply, 'I am cooking green tomato chutney using the recipe you gave me.' This can be true only if some cooking is going on, and if I did get a recipe. My reply commits me to the existence of things other than myself. 'What are you thinking about?' 'Cooking some green tomato chutney.' The reply does not imply the existence of anything other than myself – although doubtless I would not have spoken unless I thought someone was on the other end of the telephone. But what I actually say has no further existential commitment. 'What do you see?' 'It seems to me that I can make out some green tomatoes.' I have not spoken falsely if there are none around. 'Who told you to make chutney tonight?' 'God did.' I imply the existence of God. 'What are you trying to prove nowadays?' 'I am trying to prove the existence of God.' Although I indicate some hope that God exists and even that his existence can be proven, I do not thereby commit myself to the claim that my hopes will be fulfilled.

Any object that can be contemplated without existential commitment to anything except myself is, then, for me an idea. My tickles, images, concepts, seeming impressions of sense, and hoped-for proofs are all in this category. Yet surely images, tickles, and concepts are not *objects* at all?

Objects, we say, are things like carburetors, coins, and cookery books. But remember, as Foucault said of the Chinese animals, we are here a little concerned with 'the exotic charm of another system of thought'. It is not to be expected that 'objects' stay in the same place in this other system. G. E. M. Anscombe noted this in another connection:

Berkeley calls 'colours with their variations and different proportions of light and shade' the 'proper' and also the 'immediate' objects of sight . . . That word 'object' which comes in the phrase 'object of sight' has suffered a certain reversal of meaning in the history of philosophy, and so has the connected word 'subject', though the two reversals aren't historically connected. The subject used to be what the proposition, say, is about, the thing itself as it is in reality – unprocessed by being conceived, as we might say (in case there is some sort of processing there); objects on the other hand were formerly always objects *of –*. Objects of desire, objects of thought, are not objects in one common modern sense, not individual things, such as *the objects found in the accused man's pockets.*[4]

It is part of the charm (or irrelevance?) of this 'exotic system of thought' that ideas are paradigm 'objects' and coins are not. Whether material coins and cookery books are also objects is, perhaps, the main problem of metaphysics of the time. Locke answered *yes,* Berkeley *no.* I have cautiously spoken of these objects, ideas, being contemplated. That was too careful. The objectivity of ideas is only half the story. The other half has it that reasoning about ideas is like seeing. We may understand this well by reading Descartes' *Rules for the Direction of the Mind.* Although it was not published until after his death, there was a manuscript copy at Port Royal which left its imprint on the *Logic.* (Descartes himself, with his subsequent *Discourse on Method,* thought his rules had been superseded by a new technique for perfecting thought, but much of the theory of ideas found in the *Rules* persisted

---

4. 'The Intentionality of Sensation: A Grammatical Feature, in *Analytical Philosophy,* second series, ed. R. J. Butler (Oxford: Blackwell, 1968), p. 158.

throughout his work.) Descartes is unabashed in comparing thought to vision: 'Truly we shall learn how to employ our mental intuition from comparing it with the way we employ our eyes' (Rule IX). We must *look* at our ideas, "isolating them from each other and scrutinizing them separately with steadfast mental gaze'. 'Magic words' can confuse our thinking; to avoid them, get back to ideas: 'We must be content to isolate them from each other, and to give them, each of us, our individual attention, studying them with that degree of mental illumination that each of us possesses' (Rule XII).

This dead concept of mental vision is very hard for us to understand. The thought is not that ideas are like images. On the contrary, the most elevated ratiocination has objects, such as God or the will, of which we can in principle form no image. Complicated geometrical arguments have objects of which we are in fact unable to form good images. Even so, our model for understanding such concepts is to be vision. This is clear in Descartes' account of proof. It has recently been usual to think of proofs as valid in virtue of the form of the sentences that express them; perhaps Aristotle thought something like that, and certainly Leibniz urged it. But for Descartes a proof was a device that enabled a man to pluck scales from his eyes and see the truth. An angel, for example, with perfect 'mental gaze' would require no proof. Many recent philosophers of mathematics have thought that proof could be comprehended only when expressed in an appropriate formal language. Descartes, on the other hand, thought proof a device for getting rid of words, enabling a man to perceive the connections between ideas steadfastly.

Thus we must conceive ideas as the objects of mental vision (aside from a qualification to the effect that there are for example tactile images as well as visual ones). For abstract reasoning vision is the sole model, and to improve your reasoning, you need higher-powered 'illumination'. We still employ the idiom 'now I see' when an argument convinces us. Proofs after all are 'demonstrations' even now. The

Oxford English Dictionary remarks under 'see': 'As the sense of sight affords far more complete and definite information respecting external objects than any other of the senses, mental perceptions are in many (perhaps in all) languages referred to in visual terms, often with little or no consciousness of metaphor.' The lexicographers could not even refer to mental perception without the word *perception*!

The dictionary is even more misleading than appears on the surface. At least, we feel, the 'sense of sight' is a constant in the world of shifting concepts. But there is little reason to suppose that Descartes thought of eyesight as we do. The world has been turned inside out. Ideas, in the time of Descartes, were its centre. Objects have been reversed, so that what we call subjective was then called objective. We can hardly expect 'vision' to stay politely in its place. Empirically minded philosophers think of vision as lord of the senses, a superiority which is part of the very nature of man. We should not be so sure. Lucien Febvre contends that, on the basis of what is left us of emerging thirteenth-century French, those who spoke the language speak as if they lived in an auditory, olfactory universe in which objects of sight have hardly come into consciousness.[5] There is nothing in the sentences actually bequeathed us to suppose that those speakers thought of the world in a visual way (I do not support this interpretation, but its sheer shock value is important to us).

Much later the Cartesian world was thoroughly visual. Yet as Michel Foucault has urged, for Descartes and Malebranche to see with the eyes was to perceive with the mind. To reverse the dictionary just quoted, 'visual perceptions are referred to in terms of mental perception, often with little or no consciousness of metaphor'. This is true even in the case of the most concrete experience, anatomical dissection, or observation with a microscope. To perceive is, as it were, to render the object transparent. To perceive is to see *through*

5. Lucien Febvre, *Le Problemè de l'incroyance au XVI*ᵉ *siècle* (Paris: Albin Michel, 1942, 1968), Book II, Ch. 4.

something, using a light that emanates from an unassignable, original place in which the idea of the thing originates. At the end of the eighteenth century, our kind of seeing replaced that kind of perception. Objects became opaque, resisting physical light rather than admitting mental light. Cartesian perception is the active rendering of the object transparent to the mind. Positivist seeing is the passive blunting of light rays on opaque, impermeable 'physical objects' which are themselves passive and indifferent to the observer.[6]

The elements of this alien theory of ideas are as follows. First, there is a class of objects that mediate between the *ego* and the rest of the world. These objects are called ideas. Secondly, we are aware of ideas through a faculty akin to sight, or rather, of which sight is part. (Certainly ideas are not, in general, images.) Thirdly, to recall Hobbes, words signify ideas but signification is a relation of precedence–or–consequence of an almost causal sort.

It may seem that we should stop right here. This array of doctrines has nothing to do with language and cannot help us understand how language matters to philosophy. At most the task of the seventeenth-century philosopher should be to escape from the toils of language and get down to his ideas. That is mere prophylactic linguistic work, and of no general interest! Not at all: after stripping public discourse from philosophizing, one gets down to the chain of ideas, to mental discourse. That is the language that mattered to philosophy. A philosopher today may deny there is such a thing as mental discourse, and certainly he will deny that it is discourse, part of language. But it remains possible that mental discourse, utterly central to the seventeenth-century world view, played the same role then as public discourse now. Such speculation can wait. We have got some grip on ideas, at least enough grip to make us terribly cautious – so let us see what Berkeley did with them.

6. These remarks paraphrase Michel Foucault, *The Birth of the Clinic* (London: Tavistock, 1973), p. xiii.

4. Bishop Berkeley's abstractions

Berkeley was an idealist: that is, an idea-ist. He thought the only things that exist are mental. He said that he did not intend to deny anything the common man believes. Perhaps. Certainly he would not have denied that the wood was full of violets last spring. Even so it is obscure whether he would be saying what you or I say when we talk about the woods. But even if there is no difference between him and us on the topic of spring flowers he did intend to deny many things commonly said nowadays. We all believe that the world is made up, in part, of atoms and molecules. This sort of doctrine infuriated Berkeley. Such tenets of 'corpuscular philosophy', associated with Robert Boyle and turned into official English philosophy by Locke, had by 1700 conquered the minds of English intellectuals. Just possibly the 'common man' of 1700 had not yet ingested this body of theory, but it is one of the commonplaces of today and Berkeley intended to deny it.

Matter, it was supposed, is composed of tiny corpuscles. Berkeley hated matter with such a passion that J. O. Wisdom, in *The Unconscious Origin of Berkeley's Philosophy*, has connected it, by a Freudian chain, with Berkeley's bizarre obsession with practical remedies for constipation. However that may be, the matter postulated by Boyle and Locke consisted of particles with primary qualities (shape and size and motion and perhaps hardness) but no secondary qualities (colour, warmth, or taste). Secondary qualities are merely produced in us by the effect of the particles bouncing on our retinas or taste buds. Berkeley thought that the very distinction between primary and secondary qualities was an absurd mistake foisted on the world by the natural philosophy of his day. So one of the strands in Berkeley's philosophizing is an attempt to confute this distinction, and thereby undermine Locke's very conception of inert soulless colourless matter.

Another strand is the vociferous denunciation of current theories of substance, particularly, but not solely, because they invited a notion of inert corporeal substance, i.e. matter. He was eager to confute Locke's realist theory of perception, which contended that in a certain way our ideas represent something material which is outside us. Like many philosophers with a keen interest in science he thought that the latest trends were bad for faith. Corpuscular philosophy led straight to, or even entailed, atheism, but idealism would re-establish religion. At a deeper level, Berkeley is participating in a radical transformation in the concept of cause which ties up in labryinthine and fundamental ways with the concept of signification.

Like other important metaphysicians Berkeley was sensitive to each new scientific discovery and hypothesis, seeing, often in perverse ways, its interconnection with every other aspect of human life and knowledge. It was important to him to demonstrate the inadequate foundations of Newton's new differential calculus (the *Analyst,* 1734), and to reinterpret the by now established theory of mechanics (*De Motu,* 1721). It is true that his only success in these forays into natural science is with *An Essay towards a New Theory of Vision* (1709) which was called, well over a century later, 'the received theory on the subject'. His various thoughts are all of a piece and one inevitably distorts his work by following only one line of argument. Yet in the case of the relation between language and the idealist philosophy we have some license for doing so. Berkeley's masterpiece is *The Principles of Human Knowledge* (1710). It is prefaced by an Introduction almost entirely and separately devoted to one argument which, avowedly, has something to do with language:

In order to prepare the mind of the reader for the easier conceiving what follows, it is proper to premise somewhat, by way of Introduction, concerning the nature and abuse of Language. But the unravelling this matter leads me in some measure to anticipate my design, by taking notice of what seems to have had a chief part in rendering speculation intricate and perplexed, and to have occasioned innumerable errors and difficulties in almost all parts of knowledge. And that is the opinion that the mind hath a power of framing *abstract* ideas or notions of things. (sec. 6)

The problem about abstract ideas is not easily understood by us. Berkeley was indeed an idea-list; that is to say, he thoroughly accepted the concept of idea that was developed in the preceding chapter. I emphasized three elements:

(1) There is a class of objects that mediate between the *ego* and the world, and these objects are called ideas.

(2) We are aware of ideas through a faculty akin to sight, although ideas are not necessarily mere images, and the model for sight is inner 'perception' rather than outward 'seeing'.

(3) Words signify ideas, but signification is not necessarily to be construed as 'meaning', for it is a relation of precedence–consequence of an almost causal sort.

Nothing in this theory, so far, demands that a given word, say 'rain', is always, on each occasion of correct use, a sign of one and the same idea. For example, in Cambridge the afternoon drizzle elicits a muttered 'rain'; in Kampala, near the equator, the first heavy drops arouse the warning 'Rain!' as one sprints for shelter from a tropical downpour. The kind of damp outside me is different in the two cases. Equally the ideas within me, on these two occasions, may be different. They would have to be different if truth were correspondence between idea and the world. Yet the two ideas of rain ought, perhaps, to be similar, for both are ideas of rain, albeit different kinds of rain. 'Rain', said now, signifies – in Hobbes' sense of the word – my idea of the present Cambridge drizzle; in Kampala it signified my idea of those pelting drops. Thus although the word 'rain' signifies two different ideas of rain on the two occasions of use, on both occasions it signifies (in the same Hobbesian sense) ideas of rain. It does not follow (so far) that there is a single object, *the idea of rain*, which both signify.

Compare the arbitrary sign 'rain' with Hobbes' example of a natural sign, the clouds that signify the coming storm. Different formations of cumulo-nimbus signify different storms all of which are storms; equally, different utterances of 'rain' signify different ideas, all of which are ideas of rain. The meteorological association is not that every anvil-headed cloud that appears from time to time in the sky signifies some hyper-celestial object, the universal storm. At most each cloud signifies some storm or other. Likewise 'rain' need not signify the universal idea *rain*, but some idea of rain or other.

If we merely described the world, that would be the end of the matter: no universals. But we do not only report, disparage, or admire. We engage in reasoning. In working through Euclid we prove properties of triangles – all triangles. We do this (according to Descartes) by fixing the idea with 'steadfast mental gaze'. But what is the object on which to draw so steady a bead? It is certainly not some individual scalene or isosceles, for no matter how hard we stare at this slender isosceles, we can hardly be sure that the fat one has the same properties, let alone the awkward scalene next to flash upon the geometer's inward eye. Here we look not at some idea of triangle, but what is universal to triangles.

We reason about all triangles, not about what is peculiar to this or that. We cannot survey each triangle, one by one. Yet reasoning (on the theory of ideas) is like surveying. Hence we must be looking not at individual triangles, but at what is common to all triangles, and *this* commonness must itself be an object up for mental scrutiny. Thus if we stick to empirical matters, like the reporting of rain, we may say that utterances of 'rain' signify some idea of rain or other and we need not postulate something common to all ideas of rain, but when we turn to the *a priori*, we require an object whose features are exactly what is common to all triangles. Naturally there can be no image of such a thing, but there may still be an abstract idea of a triangle. Mountaineers reporting triangular eminences have no need to postulate what is common to all triangles, but geometers who believe in an ego with ideas and believe that the ego looks at ideas, must postulate an idea looked at when reasoning about triangles, and no idea of a particular triangle will do. Finally: if words signify ideas, then once we have got an abstract idea of a triangle that is a handy thing for the word 'triangle' to signify. And since we do have the faculty of forming abstract ideas, then perchance we have an abstract idea of 'rain' too. Plato, our original idea-man, made geometry a prerequisite for academic study. In a later era it was certainly essential for belief in abstract ideas.

To repeat: the three elements of the seventeenth-century doctrine of ideas are: (1) The ego has ideas to mediate between inner and outer; (2) Perception is the model for knowledge of ideas; (3) Words signify ideas. The geometer adds the fourth, optional, extra: (4) There are abstract ideas which are the objects of 'mental vision'. Berkeley accepts the whole doctrine of ideas except for (4), which (as we have seen from the quotation earlier in this chapter) he believed to be the root of philosophical evil.

Many modern commentators have taken Berkeley to be chiefly concerned with 'the problem of universals'. There are a great many problems that philosophers have, from time to time, called 'problems about universals'. One of the favourites nowadays is the question of how it is possible for general terms to have meaning. For example, it is tempting to suppose that a general word (like 'rain') gets its meaning from, or actually means, what all rain has in common. Against this view Wittgenstein, it is said, postulated that some terms get their meaning from 'family resemblances'. There is nothing in common to all games, but there is a chain of resemblances, a cluster of properties, or some such, that connects patience and rugby football, chess and the pentathlon, war games by the NATO fleet and ring-around-a-rosy. Such questions about general terms are indeed of interest. Perhaps they are central to some of Plato's thought. But we may usefully recall Kant's rude remarks about how the seventeenth-century notion of *idea* is altogether different from the Platonic one from which, etymologically, it derives. Berkeley saw clearly that there is nothing in the seventeenth-century doctrine of ideas that implies anything about the meaning of general terms – nothing, that is, except the theory of geometrical proof as mental vision which requires an object. So I believe that much modern commentary misdirects us. This is certainly confirmed by Berkeley's own Introduction. It is worried about the way general terms occur in proofs. He tries to explain how we can reason geometrically without having an abstract idea to contemplate. In a proof, he claims, we can arrive at a general conclusion even though, at certain stages in the reasoning, we have only an idea of a particular triangle to reason about. Modern logic, especially in a format called 'Natural Deduction', invented by Gerhard Gentzen in the 1930s, may provide a formal confirmation and analysis of Berkeley's conception of proof by particulars.

We are not here concerned with how sound Berkeley's argument is, nor whether it has finally been vindicated by symbolic logic, but simply with discovering what the argument is. When you read Berkeley's Introduction, you should be struck by a surprising absence. Berkeley never *argues* that there are no abstract ideas! There is a good deal of rhetoric. He scornfully refers to 'this wonderful faculty of abstracting' alleged by Locke and his peers, but contempt is no argument. Instead, Berkeley quite simply says,

I deny that I can abstract from one another, or conceive separately, those qualities which it is impossible should exist so separated; or that I can frame a general notion by abstracting from particulars in the manner aforesaid. (sec. 10)

For example, a triangle cannot exist without being scalene or isosceles; no more can we conceive such a thing, so Berkeley finds in himself no such abstract idea, no triangle, neither scalene nor isosceles.

If any man has the faculty of framing in his mind such an idea of a triangle as is here described, *it is in vain to pretend to dispute him out of it, nor would I go about it.* (*sec.* 13, my italics)

Why does Berkeley decline to argue? Because he accepts thesis (2) of the doctrine of ideas, that ideas are the objects of a faculty akin to sight. To discover if one has abstract ideas 'can be no hard task for anyone to perform. What more easy than for any one to look a little into his own thoughts, and there try whether he has, or can attain to have, an idea' of a general triangle (sec. 13). Berkeley does not argue because there can be no point in arguing about something one can discover by direct inspection.

Modern readers usually suppose that Berkeley wants our introspection to fail to turn up an image of an abstract triangle. This is not what he is after. He acknowledges plenty of ideas of which we can form no images, God and the will, for example. He is denying that the faculty akin to sight, and which has ideas as objects, has any abstract ideas as objects. He moreover argues (and this is his only argument in this connection) that we have no need for such objects in geometrical demonstration.

It must be hard to see how the discussion of abstract ideas can possibly establish the idealist maxim that to be is to be perceived. Yet the *tour de force* is almost complete. Remember Descartes telling us to avoid 'magic words' and get back to ideas. So long as we focus on ideas we cannot go wrong. Berkeley has a particularly trenchant statement of this widely held opinion:

So long as I confine my thoughts to my own ideas, divested of words, I do not see how I can easily be mistaken. The objects I consider, I clearly and adequately know. I cannot be deceived in thinking I have an idea which I have not. (sec. 22)

I can utter the words 'triangle neither scalene nor isosceles' or, worse, 'what is common to all triangles'. But those are only words. When I attend to my ideas, there is nothing answering to those seductive words, and I shall resist seduction. This sensible way of keeping to virgin thought had been imperilled by the lure of mathematics, but that is now discredited. We can now, implies Berkeley, briskly settle other abuses of the notion of abstraction.

Consider the words 'thing that exists even though it is not an object of thought'. The construction is just as grammatical as 'triangle that is not any particular scalene nor isosceles'. Looking inwards we found no idea corresponding to these words. Public discourse could string the syllables together, but in mental discourse, freed of words, there is nothing corresponding. What about unthought existents? The only way in which I can discover if there is an idea corresponding to the words 'unthought existent' is to look inward, seeking for a corresponding object. But any object that we find in thought is an object of thought. So we shall never find an idea represented by the words 'thing that exists even though it is not an object of thought'. Hence that piece of public discourse is a string of empty words. Everything that exists must be a present object of thought. Present objects of thought are perceived. (Not *seen*, in the sense that emerged in the eighteenth century, but *perceived*, in the Cartesian sense described in the last chapter.) To be is to be perceived.

This proof, widely regarded as the most preposterous argument ever to achieve lasting fame among philosophers, seems to me very impressive. Within the conceptual scheme in which it is formulated, the steps seem to me cogent (not incontestable, of course, but cogent). Moreover, unlike much philosophy it does what is wanted. By the time we have got into the language of idea/object/perception, we recognize that it is correct to assert, 'There were lots of violets in the wood this spring.' Berkeley's truth-conditions for this statement will strike the mean-minded philosopher as strange, but it comes out just as true for Berkeley as for the man of more mundane conceptions. On the other hand, the atoms and molecules of corpuscular philosophy, the very substance of matter, can now only be deemed the merest dust raised by natural philosophers whose atheistic tendencies are heightened by the perversions of public language. Like a cleansing shower on a hot summer's day, idealism lays this dust to rest.

There are, as I have said at the beginning, lots of other arguments, having nothing to do with language, with which Berkeley strives to establish idealism. But here we have an argument, thought valuable enough to introduce the reader to the *Principles*, and which avowedly begins with language. It is a particularly important argument, for it is logical or metaphysical in character. Many of Berkeley's other arguments for idealism are epistemological, having to do with how we know things. They are culled from sixteenth-century sceptics. But the argument from language is rather new. Since its chief aim is showing that we are misled by language, it may seem to be a merely prophylactic application of linguistic theory to philosophy. That is, it looks like one of those uses of language which, in my first chapter, I described as of minor interest. We are in a conceptual mess, Berkeley thinks, so we had better get clear about language and then proceed to do some sound philosophy. This is not, however, the whole story. Certainly Berkeley does not write like someone saying that by 'free will' we mean two things or nine things or nothing. Berkeley's central doctrine about language is that *if I confine my thoughts to my own ideas, divested of words*, I cannot easily go wrong. The chain of my ideas forms mental discourse, logically prior to the public discourse that leads us astray. If we understand 'language' as broadly as possible, so that it includes all discourse, then it was not only his negative view about public discourse that mattered to Berkeley's philosophy. His positive doctrine on mental discourse was crucial to the argument of the Introduction.

5. Nobody's theory of meaning

Despite the excellence of Alston's classification of theories of meaning – ideational, referential, behavioural – we have seen how curiously difficult it is to pin any one of these on Hobbes and others. Yet we often experience little difficulty applying the same categories to modern philosophers. There is, I think, a good explanation. There is a proper sense of 'theory of meaning', which I shall now elucidate, in which none of our early empiricists undertook to provide well-worked-out theories of meaning at all. They did make many remarks which can variously be construed as supporting ideational, referential, or behavioural theories of meaning. But what modern philosophers call the theory of meaning did not matter much to them. Language did, avowedly, matter, but not necessarily in the ways that it has mattered of late. Our contemporaries often equate 'philosophy of language' and 'theory of meaning'. At best, that is a poor anachronism to bring to historical studies; at worst, it is misguided even for current philosophical analysis. Language matters, but I suspect that meaning does not.

Let us have one more battle with the theory of ideas. It is intimately connected with language, for 'words signify ideas'. If this doctrine were an ideational theory of meaning then the meaning of a word would be an idea; the meaning of a sentence, a thought that combines ideas or perhaps such a thought would itself be an idea. One job for spoken language is communication: I have mental discourse; so do you. I speak aloud, and thereby produce in you some intended mental discourse. One could, with Jonathan Bennett, call this a 'translation view of language'. I translate my mental discourse into spoken words, which you hear and retranslate into mental discourse.[1]

It would seem essential to a translational view combined with an ideational theory that quite frequently the double translation succeeds. That is, you ought to end up with the same ideas in your breast that I have in mine. This does not mean that you have to agree with what I say. I mutter, 'The coffee is horrid.' You disagree. But at least, it appears, you have formed the same chain of ideas (*nasty + coffee*) that I had in mind when I said that the coffee is horrid. We disagree on the quality of the coffee but we know what we are talking about. On the translation view of language, I had a chain of ideas in my breast, I translated them into words, and you translated them back into a string of ideas in your breast.

But how do I know you have the same ideas as me? I cannot look into your mind. The ideational-translator ought to tell us the criteria of identity for ideas in the minds of several speakers. Locke undoubtedly says in the *Essay* (III.ii.8) 'that unless a man's words excite the same ideas in the hearer which he makes them stand for in speaking, he does not speak intelligibly'. Surely Locke ought to define 'same idea' and then prove that in many cases of successful communication, the same idea is produced in the listener as was present to the speaker. Notoriously, none of our old philosophers bothers to give such a definition, or proves interpersonal identity of ideas. Hence either they were not 'ideational-translators', or else they were unusually unreflective.

Locke does have something to say about identity of ideas, but not in connection with language. He wonders in a case of straightforward perception, if it is possible that '*the same object should produce in several men's minds different ideas*

1. J. F. Bennett, *Locke, Berkeley, Hume: Central Themes* (Oxford: University Press, 1971), p. 1.

at the same time' (*Essay*, II.xxxii.15). His own example is vivid; he asks what if 'the idea that a violet produced in one man's mind by his eyes were the same that a marigold produced in another man's'. This is, incidentally, not just an example of colour. The wild marigolds now running riot in my field are a coarse bold shade of orange. Earlier this year the violets in Knapwell wood were delicate, soft beneath the subtle green foliage. The poet's 'bashful' fits that flower. The marigolds are brazen. The contrast is not only of colour but of character.

The question is not whether when I say, 'Look at the marigolds', you form the picture that I form when I look at violets. Locke wonders if, when we both look at my summer field, and each achieves an idea of flowers, your idea is unlike mine, although much the same as the idea I get on strolling through the wood in early spring. Having presented the question in a singularly graphic way, Locke proceeds to dismiss it. He doubts that this sort of thing ever happens. Moreover he thinks it useless to pursue the question. Anyway, he continues, if on looking at my marigolds you did have an idea that I would call a violet-idea no falsehood would ensue, for there would be no confounding of your idea with mine.

The last observation is crucial. In those days the confounding of ideas was supposed to be the source of error, and indeed, the sole source of error. Such a doctrine is the inevitable consequence of the Cartesian ego, to whom only ideas are present, and from which anything about the rest of the word can only be inferred non-deductively. The only evidence we have lies in our ideas. Therefore they are our only source of error. As we have seen, the doctrine that we study our ideas with steadfast mental gaze was bequeathed by Descartes to the Port Royal *Logic*, and swallowed almost whole by the British disciples. Falsehood cannot arise from *you* having what *I* would call a violet-idea when you see marigolds because it is only *my* ideas that mediate between what is within me and what is outside.

It follows that the question about ideas of violets and marigolds is of little importance to seventeenth-century epistemology, which is concerned, egotistically, with my ideas and with the world. We can also understand why Locke, though judging the issue unimportant, still thinks it likely that you do get what I would call a marigold-idea when you look at marigolds. For he also accepts the Cartesian doctrine that perceptions of sense involve particles bouncing off objects and hitting nerve ends, which in turn transmit messages to the brain according to purely physical principles. He is hazy as to how those physical impulses produce ideas of colour, but doubtless by something law-like; unless we have grounds for supposing that your physiology and your psychology differ from mine, we can think it likely that the same laws of physics and of the psyche operate in both cases, producing similar effects from similar causes. The marigolds out there will produce an idea in your mind similar to the one it produces in mine. But that, to repeat, is not central to the epistemology of the Cartesian *ego*. Descartes himself, as we shall see in the next chapter, found the change from brain-impulses to ideas of colour so inexplicable that he supposed us to have an innate faculty that produces our ideas of colours for us. Locke had quite the opposite opinion.

Given Locke's problem areas, his dismissal of the violet marigold problem seems to me correct. Bennett on the contrary speaks of Locke's 'complacency' and, quoting the cursory treatment of marigolds, says, 'the incoherence of this shows Locke's failure to see the depth of his difficulty' for the theory of meaning. I propose that Locke does not have a difficulty, because he is not interested in the theory of meaning at all. Another passage illustrates this. He says that although words 'can properly and immediately signify nothing but the ideas that are in the mind of the speaker', in their thoughts 'men *give them a secret reference* to two other things'. One of these secret references is '*the reality of things*'. In the other 'secret reference' men

suppose their words to be marks of the ideas in the minds also of other men, with whom they communicate: for else they should talk in vain, and could not be understood, if the sounds they applied to one idea were such as by the hearer were applied to another, which is to speak two languages. But in this men stand not usually to examine, whether the idea they, and those they discourse with have in their minds be the same: but think it enough that they use the word, as they imagine, in the common acceptation of that language. (III.ii.4)

Does Locke support this doctrine of 'secret reference'? I think the very phrase is loaded with Locke's characteristic irony. 'Give me leave here to say', he continues in case anyone has failed to take the point, "it is a perverting the use of words, and brings unavoidable obscurity and confusion into their signification, whenever we make them stand for anything but those ideas we have in our own minds.' Signifying, remember, is a relation of precedence–or–consequence. So what Locke says seems correct. Note that another term is used in this passage, 'the common acceptation' of a word in a language. This is something quite different from signifying. Let us take, for example, the role of a name in some speech. Had the real Mark Antony said, 'I come to bury Caesar, not to praise him', there would have been the idea of Caesar present in Mark Antony's mind. That is what the name 'Caesar' signifies, for Antony. The third plebeian, despite the inane responses Shakespeare puts in his mouth, doubtless also has some idea (possibly not Antony's) of Caesar. That is what the name signifies for him. In contrast, there is the actual person referred to, recently deceased. Finally there is, perhaps, something else in the public domain: everyone realizes that Rome's tyrant is under discussion. This shared cognition we might, borrowing Locke's phrase, call the common acceptation of the name 'Caesar'. Common acceptation enables Antony to address the multitude. It is whatever is 'public' about the established use of a word.

Common acceptation is not 'proper and immediate signification'. According to Bennett, Locke 'genuinely does not distinguish' the two questions,

(a) Do you mean by 'violet' what I do?
(b) Do violet things sensorily affect you as they do me?

Locke 'takes them to be two versions of the single univocal question', namely,

(c) Are your ideas of violet the same as mine?[2]

I think the situation is more complicated, for Locke does not use the word 'mean'. Let us consider three questions in place of Bennett's single 'Do you mean by "violet" what I do?' We replace meaning in (a) successively by signification, reference, and common acceptation.

(a1) Does 'violet' *signify* the same idea for you as it does for me?
(a2) When I say, now, 'the first violet to bloom in the garden this spring', am I *referring* to the same plant as you refer to, uttering the same words, here and now?
(a3) In your community, does 'violet' have the same *common acceptation* as in mine?

Compare Bennett's other question: 'Do violet things sensorily affect you as they do me?' and gloss this as,

(b1) When you notice them, do violets produce the same idea in you as they do in me, when I am examining them?

Bennett is right in saying that Locke fails to distinguish two questions. The questions which Locke fails to distinguish are (a1) and (b1). These two questions are, of course, different, because you might not ever have heard the word 'violet' before – you might be a unilingual Russian – and so the word 'violet' would signify nothing at all to you. But leave such quibbles aside: we are concerned with English-speaking communities. Then although (a1) and (b1) remain different,

2. Op. cit., p. 7, n. 1.

they at least obtain parallel or identical answers except in further cases of quibbling (colour-blindness, say). I do not think much would hang on a failure to make a sharp distinction between (a1) and (b1).

Bennett, however, does not mean 'signify' by 'mean'. He means what Locke calls common acceptation. Thus he is accusing Locke of equating (a3) and (b1), not (a1) and (b1). Locke makes no such confusion. Bennett's mistake is easy enough to make – for us, 'signify' can mean 'mean'; a theory of signification is therefore a theory of meaning, and a theory of meaning, for Bennett, is a theory of common acceptation. But Locke has no theory of common acceptation at all. I agree, however, that Locke did not guard himself against Bennett's reading. The distinctions required were not made efficiently until the late nineteenth century, when Gottlob Frege had to legislate a distinction into the German language in order to avoid confusion. He took the word *Sinn* – which has been translated 'meaning' but in English is nowadays called 'sense' – as common acceptation. By way of contrast he used the word *Bedeutung* – equally translated 'meaning' but now fixed with the English word 'reference'.

The regular connexion between a sign, its sense, and its reference is of such a kind that to the sign there corresponds a definite sense and to that in turn a definite reference, while to a given reference (an object) there does not belong only a single sign. The same sense has different expressions in different languages or even in the same language.[3]

Frege also considers something analogous to what Locke would have called the idea signified by a sign. Frege speaks of the 'idea' associated with a word, in contrast to the word's sense and reference. There has been much philosophy between Locke and Frege, and the word 'idea' has not stayed

3. On 'Sense and Reference' in *Translations from the Philosophical Writings of Gottlob Frege*, ed. P. Geach and M. Black (Oxford: Blackwell, 1952), p. 58.

in its place, especially when translated into German as *Vor-stellung* and back again. But enough has been preserved to take the continuation of this translated passage as read:

The reference and sense of a sign are to be distinguished from the associated idea. If the reference of a sign is an object perceivable by the senses, my idea of it is an internal image, arising from memories of sense impressions which I have had and acts, both internal and external, which I have performed. Such an idea is often saturated with feeling; the clarity of its separate parts varies and oscillates. The same sense is not always connected, even in the same man, with the same idea. The idea is subjective: one man's idea is not that of another. There result, as a matter of course, a variety of differences in the ideas associated with the same sense. A painter, a horseman, and a zoologist will probably connect different ideas with the name 'Bucephalus'. This constitutes an essential distinction between the idea and the sign's sense, which may be the common property of many and therefore is not a part of a mode of the individual mind. For one can hardly deny that mankind has a common store of thoughts which is transmitted from one generation to another.[4]

Henceforth I shall use the phrase 'theory of meaning' to mean something that at least includes a theory of what Frege called 'sense' (*Sinn*) and what Locke may have called common acceptation. That is, theories of meaning have to do with the essentially public features of language, with whatever it is that is common to you and me, in respect of the word 'violet', which makes it possible for us to talk about the flowers in Knapwell wood. Frege was sure there had to be *Sinn* because *a common store of thoughts and propositions is transmitted from one generation to the other.*

Readers who are trained chiefly in the exacting disciplines of analytic philosophy will find it quite natural to use Frege's words to characterize our category 'theory of meaning', but it will seem strange to anyone else. We may forget that at the time Frege was writing, meanings were on the rampage. In his day nearly every discipline had a critique based on meanings

4. *Ibid.* pp. 58-9.

or else a theory about them. In 1881 the American physicist J. B. Stallo was confuting the atomic theory of matter from the vantage point of a phenomenalist theory of meanings; Ernst Mach deployed a similar analysis on all branches of physics. Max Weber, the great founding theoretician of modern sociology, begins his analysis by distinguishing the objective and subjective meanings of an action. Freud's psychoanalysis is nothing other than a theory of meanings. And so on: meanings were everywhere and Frege, despite his focus on words, sentences, and verbal communication, is only one of many agents who participated in the heyday of meanings.

I use Frege to designate a specific kind of interest in meaning that has become dominant in one branch of philosophy, just as I might use Weber to characterize a certain concern with meanings that has preoccupied one limb of sociology. Although Weber and Frege (and Freud and Mach) start with the same German vocabulary of *Sinn* and *Bedeutung*, they direct it in different ways. When I speak of a theory of meaning in this book, I fix on Frege. Were this a less insular enquiry we could hardly use so narrow a specification. I use it because my case studies are all drawn from one kind of philosophical analysis. All the examples of subsequent chapters have strong lines of filiation to Frege. Our culture quite properly does not attach so specific a meaning to 'meaning' as analytic philosophers do. One has heard of an undergraduate course advertised as 'The meaning of life'; the throngs of students were dismayed to learn it was about the meaning of the word 'life'. It is poor taste to play such tricks by punning on meaning, but in what follows it is unexceptionable to employ Frege's peculiar delimitation of the field.

Frege, like all his contemporaries, saw that public communication cannot be well explained by what he called private associated ideas. Locke, and *his* contemporaries, did not see this at all clearly. Nor did Locke and his friends care. He undoubtedly thought that whenever we do communicate successfully, you get the same ideas in your breast as I have in mine. But in the works of Locke this notion is not part of a philosophical theory of communication. It is almost a physical conjecture about how external stimuli produce ideas in the mind: doubtless they do this in some regular way, so that the same external stimuli will produce similar internal effects. So if you associate an idea with the word 'gold' that is different from the idea I associate with it, we are probably, as a matter of physics and psychology, miscommunicating. This Lockean opinion about communication may be rubbish, as some modern philosophers contend. But as Locke makes absolutely plain in his brief ironic remarks, the theory of public communication (of common acceptation or *Sinn*) is of no importance to his philosophy. Locke did not have a theory of meaning. He did not have a theory of public discourse. He had a theory of ideas. That is a theory of mental discourse.

I have laboured this point to illustrate a paradox. It is widely held among modern analytic philosophers that such writers as Locke and Berkeley are interested in the same fundamental problems of metaphysics and epistemology that plague us today. Furthermore, it is held that their approaches to these problems are determined by their theories of meaning. I argue that those philosophers had no theories of meaning, in the sense now given to that phrase. There are three possibilities. (1) I may be wrong; they had theories of meaning. (2) Locke and Berkeley were not working on our problems of metaphysics and epistemology. (3) They were working on something structurally similar to our problems, but in which the slot now allotted to what is public was then filled by something private. I shall urge that the third answer is correct. When mental discourse was taken for granted, ideas were the interface between the Cartesian *ego* and reality. We have displaced mental discourse by public discourse, and 'ideas' have become unintelligible. Something in the domain of public discourse now serves as the interface between the knowing subject and the world. Thus in my opinion the seventeenth-century writers do not help us answer the question 'Why does language matter to philosophy?' by what they say about theory of meaning. On the contrary, I shall take the *absence* of a theory of meaning as part of the data for understanding why language matters to philosophy today. My first four case studies are ones in which mental discourse matters and there is *no* theory of meaning. The next step is to have a collection of studies in which public discourse matters and there *is* a theory of meaning. We heighten the contrast by jumping a couple of centuries.

B. The heyday of meaning

6. Noam Chomsky's innatism

We now pass over two centuries of vivid and intense philosophical speculation. We leave the seventeenth century, the
era of ideas, and find ourselves in the early twentieth century,
the time when 'meanings' seem to preoccupy philosophy. The
remarks of Frege quoted in the preceding chapter indicate
what has happened, quite universally. He cares about *Sinn*,
public meaning, the transmitter of the store of thoughts from
one generation to the next. The associated idea, private
mediator between the lonely ego and the larger world, is of
no interest at all. As a transition between the seventeenth-
century world and the recent one, it is convenient to start
with a deliberate throwback. In the past decade the linguist
Noam Chomsky has revived an old controversy about innate
ideas. I shall try to describe some of the roles it played in seventeenth-century thought, and how Chomsky tried to re-
deploy it.

Although immense passions have been raised on either
side, as much in 1960 as in 1690, it is often obscure, to the
bystander, exactly what is at issue. It is almost as if the
phrase 'innate ideas' were a symbolic masthead, of no importance at all in itself, but furnishing a rallying point for embat-
tled legions who are fighting about something far more important. But this is not the view of the protagonists themselves:

Our differences are on subjects of some importance. The question
is to know whether, following Aristotle and [Locke], the soul in
itself is entirely empty, like a tablet on which nothing has yet

been written (*tabula rasa*), and whether all that is traced thereon comes solely from the senses and from experience; or whether as I, with Plato, believe, the soul contains originally the principles of several notions and doctrines which external objects merely awaken on occasions.[1]

Perhaps we had best begin by asking how children learn to talk. This question sounds innocently experimental. To answer it, study infants beginning to speak. Yet some question like this has repeatedly intervened in philosophy. Different answers are supposed to represent fundamentally different views about human nature and to characterize deep differences between rationalists and empiricists.

The two most enduring models of language acquisition are best introduced by two old metaphors. There is the 'blank slate' (or table of wax) to which Locke, in Book I of the *Essay Concerning Human Understanding* compares the infant newly brought into the world. Knowing nothing, the wax passively waits for experience to write upon it. Then there is the 'block of marble' employed by Leibniz in his *New Essays*, attacking Locke: the child, like marble, is grained, so that only some shapes can be hewn from it by experience. The child is born with the form of possible concepts innate within it.

The empiricist 'blank slate' theory commits one to the view that all knowledge is gained from experience. This includes not only knowledge of what is true, but also knowledge of how to do things, including classifying and talking. In the beginning, so runs the theory, babies merely experience. But their experiences differ. The presence of mother feels different from her absence. Hunger differs from a full stomach. Noting these differences the infant forms ideas of mother and of hunger, that is to say, it bawls in its pram when waking alone

1. G. W. Leibniz, *New Essays Concerning Human Understanding*, preface, para. 3 (written by 1703). Trans. A. G. Langley (LaSalle, Ill.: Open Court, 1916).

four hours after the last feed. Later it learns to say, 'Hungry mummy' and finally, 'More pie mother please.'

Three of the elements of learning words are, then: noting features given by experience; noting how these features match some sounds uttered by elders; and uttering sounds corresponding to features in ways that pass muster by society. These are only three of the elements. Learning to speak means learning to utter sentences in various moods, not just uttering a word in the presence of a feature. Perhaps you say, 'Hungry!' only when you are hungry, so 'Hungry' matches presence of hunger, but likely 'More pie!' matches absence of more pie. Learning grammar is at least as important as learning words. The empiricist contends not that learning words is the whole of learning language, but that it is the beginning, and it is the right place to start a theory.

One part of the starting point will be what Peter Geach calls abstractionism – 'the doctrine that a concept is acquired by a process of singling out in attention some one feature given in direct experience – *abstracting* it – and ignoring other features simultaneously given – *abstracting from* them'.[2] Another part of at least a naive empiricist theory is that the infant is not born with a selective abstracting device, making it attend to particular features; it simply notices whatever features are in fact differentiated before it. A human blank slate put into a wholly alien universe would not make the sortings peculiarly useful to us. Perhaps it would still bawl four hours after its last feed, but if it managed to survive on a diet of nectar of snapdragons fed to it by an oceanic pulsing rhomboid, it would not have the idea of mother. It would not even have a 'disposition' to have the idea of mother, no more than our children have a disposition to respond to the opalescent feeder-figure so essential to life in that other imagined universe.

2. *Mental Acts* (London: Routledge and Kegan Paul, [n.d.]), p. 18.

The rationalist's analogy of a chunk of marble derives from the fact that marble has veins. They may not determine one to sculpt the Virgin rather than Ulysses S. Grant, but at least they preclude you from making a model of a 1927 Stutz Bearcat. Less metaphorically, the infant is predisposed to notice certain features, and only some kinds of ideas can be formed in it by experience. Infants are born with a tendency to howl when hungry; they are also born with a tendency to pick out mother, hunger, colours, triangles, and even shapes as peculiar as combs, each at definite stages of maturation. Later come relations of order, 'left-right' and much else. In saying that ideas are innate, the rationalist does not contend that an ability to discriminate is actually present in the mind of every child. Rather the word 'innate' is used, says Descartes,

in the same sense [in which] we say that in some families generosity is innate, in others certain diseases like gout or gravel, not that on this account the babes of these families suffer from these diseases in their mother's womb, but because they are born with a certain disposition or propensity for contracting them.[3]

This talk of 'disposition or propensity' makes it a little hard to see what is actually at issue between blank slate and block marble. Locke, our empiricist, says on the first page of his *Essay* that he aims only at showing that our knowledge derives from our 'Natural faculties'. Why should it not be, as the rationalist suggests, a natural faculty to sort things into mothers and triangles? Later in the first chapter (sec. 22) Locke considers implicit and explicit understanding: 'it will be hard to conceive what is meant by a principle imprinted on the understanding implicitly, unless it be this, – that the mind is capable of understanding and assenting'. When we find our protagonists quarrelling between 'propensity' on the one hand

---

3. *Notes directed against a Certain Programme*, trans. E. S. Haldane and G. R. T. Ross in *The Philosophical Works of Descartes* (Cambridge: University Press, 1911), I, p. 442.

and 'capability' on the other, we may tend to think it is all a matter of words. The rationalist, believing we have innate ideas, does not contend that children can display mastery of a concept either before appropriate experience has elicited it or before the right stage of maturity is reached. The empiricist does not deny that we have a natural faculty for abstracting ideas from presentations of just those features that are important to people. It seems that there can be no real dispute. Yet great matters were at stake. I shall describe two, one from the philosophy of perception, one from the philosophy of mathematics, and then discuss one more that has excited much recent controversy. When we remain at the level of the pure theory of language acquisition, the argument between innatist and empiricist fades, but when we consider the applications to philosophy it regains its importance.

Descartes' advocacy of innate ideas had several motives including his novel proof of the existence of God given in the third *Meditation*. He also had a radical refutation of empiricist doctrine. Locke says we abstract from features such as colour and shape that are presented to us. Descartes contends that no such features are ever presented. The world with its features impinges on us by little particles bouncing off nerve ends. But the perception of red is utterly different from bouncing particles. The feeling of hunger bears no resemblance to enzymes secreting. 'No ideas of things in the shape we envisage them by thought, are presented to us by the senses . . . for nothing reaches our mind from external objects through the organs of sense beyond certain corporeal movements.'[4]

Hence it follows that the ideas of the movements and figures are themselves innate in us. So much the more must the ideas of pain, colour, sound and the like be innate, that our mind may, on occasion of certain corporeal movements, envisage these ideas, for they have no likeness to the corporeal movements.[5]

4. *Ibid.* p. 442.
5. *Ibid.* p. 443.

This argument, based on a remarkable theory about the nature of perception, is backed up by something more commonplace. We have the idea of a geometrical triangle, but 'when first in infancy we see a triangular figure depicted on paper, this figure cannot show how a real triangle ought to be conceived', because the lines that we see are not exactly straight.

But because we already possess within us the idea of a true triangle, and because it can be more easily conceived by our mind than the more complex figure of the triangle drawn on paper, we, therefore, when we see that composite figure apprehend not it itself but rather the authentic triangle.[6]

The triangle reminds us of another argument for innateness familiar since Plato's *Meno* (82–7). Socrates asked a boy how to construct a square double the size of a given square. At first the boy gave wrong answers, but after a period of delicate questioning he was able to discover the secret for himself. He neither measured nor surveyed but rather let his mind follow the appropriate route and so come upon the correct solution. Socrates argues that since the boy did not learn the answer from experience, he must have had it within him all the time. From Plato's time onwards the influence of the philosophy of mathematics on Western philosophy has been out of all proportion. Philosophers have been constantly perplexed that some knowledge can be a *priori* – can be attained independent of experience, like the slave boy's theorem on doubling squares. 'If some events can be foreseen', writes Leibniz, 'before any trial has been made of them, it is manifest that we must contribute something of our own thereto' (Preface to the *New Essays*).

Not only does proof enable us to 'foresee' properties of shapes and numbers but also the discoveries made in mathematics seem possessed of a universal necessity. They cannot

6. 'Reply to Objections V', trans. Haldane and Ross, *Philosophical Works of Descartes*, ii, pp. 227-8.

possibly be false. Not even an omnipotent God could construct a world in which they are false. We can hardly learn this from experience, for 'the senses', as Leibniz continues,

... never give anything but examples, that is to say, particular or individual truths. Now all the examples which confirm a general truth, however numerous they be, do not suffice to establish the universal necessity of this same truth. Whence it would seem that necessary truths such as are found in pure mathematics and especially in arithmetic and in geometry, must have principles the proof of which does not depend on examples, nor, consequently, on the testimony of the senses, although without the senses we would never take it into our heads to think of them.

Mathematical theorems may seem a long way from learning the meaning of words. The connection is as follows. Suppose that we could, *pace* Descartes, abstract the 'authentic figure' of a geometrical triangle from experience. Once an able geometer has this idea he can prove without further experiment all sorts of facts about triangles. The idea of triangle, which he possesses, is the idea of triangle necessarily having all those properties to which Pythagoras, Euclid, Hilbert, *et al.* have drawn our attention, and indeed many more properties to be published in next year's mathematical journals. It would be ludicrous, says the rationalist, to suppose that in learning the word 'triangle' we abstract all those aspects from experience. Hence the idea of a geometrical triangle is not got by abstraction. Only innate ideas can explain necessary truths and *a priori* knowledge.

The differences between Locke and innatists are, as Leibniz says, 'on subjects of some importance'. Consider the danger of holding, with Descartes, that ideas of shapes and of colour are innate, albeit elicited by particles bouncing off nerve ends. The realist philosopher of perception wants to say that true ideas of the world 'resemble' the real world; indeed it is this resemblance that constitutes truth. After Descartes, Berkeley is waiting in the wings to retort, 'An idea is like nothing but an idea!' So true ideas do not correspond to the material world. Locke's theory of perception is dismissed. Belief in a material world is undermined. Berkeleyian idealism is rampant.

Problems about perception and about mathematics which so exercised Descartes, Locke, Leibniz, and Berkeley are still with us, but we tend to treat them in different ways. Innate ideas have recently been of interest to philosophers for another reason, a fundamental doubt about the very possibility of abstraction. I have used Geach's definition of 'abstractionism' above. His 'own view is that abstractionism is wholly mistaken; that no concept at all is acquired by the supposed process of abstraction'. The conclusion is Cartesian, but the reasons given are not.

The blank slate theory has the infant noticing that several experiences or sensations are alike. But field poppies and cheap lipstick differ. They are also similar in colour. There is no such thing as being simply 'alike' or 'the same' or 'similar – there is only similarity in some respect or other. Hence, it is argued, the child cannot acquire colour concepts by noting some similarity between the lipstick and the poppy; it must notice that the two are alike-in-respect-of-colour. But how, it is asked, can one notice this unless one has a concept of colour in the first place?

Imagine that notwithstanding we can abstract 'pure' similarity. We are supposed to attend to some 'feature' exhibited by various objects. Geach reminds us of the concept of chromatic colour – 'real' colour, *i.e.* colour other than grey or white or black. A poppy field does not exhibit the feature of redness independent of being chromatically coloured. It is simultaneously red *and* chromatically coloured. There is no single unequivocal feature there in the world before us from which we are to abstract redness alone.

This point can be intensified by using a trick that Nelson Goodman devised for another purpose.[7] An object is what he

7. *Fact, Fiction and Forecast* (Cambridge, Mass.: Harvard University Press, 1951).

calls 'grue' if it is green and examined before 1984, or is not examined before 1984 and is blue. Anything you show me today which is green is also grue. Anything we examine today which is not green also fails to be grue. Yet according to the abstractionist it is from examples of green that we abstract the idea of green. Green is certainly not the same property as grue. I expect that an emerald unearthed in 1990 will be green and not grue. But I cannot today point to anything visible that exhibits the property of greenness and not that of grueness. Despite this we all presume that just one feature is grasped from today's examples, namely the feature that we call green. Yet any set of examples furnished for abstraction will offer too many features. The examples *underdetermine* the quality, greenness, that we are supposed to abstract from them. Despite the fact that grue and green are not perennially co-extensive there are always many qualities, such as grueness, possessed by all the available examples of greenness and not possessed by any present ungreen thing.

The fact that the environment underdetermines what is learned from it is not necessarily at odds with 'the latter day attitudes that are associated with the name of empiricism, of behaviourism', which according to W.v.O. Quine, one of the most distinguished advocates of those attitudes, is 'up to its neck in innate mechanisms of learning-readiness'.

The very reinforcement and extinction of responses, so central to behaviorism, depends on prior inequalities in the subject's qualitative spacing, so to speak, of stimulations . . . Since each learned response presupposes some such prior inequalities, some such inequalities must be unlearned; hence innate. Innate biases and dispositions are the cornerstone of behaviorism.[8]

Some readers will have more sympathy with Goodman's defence of a more robust empiricism, which denies that any talk of propensities, tendencies, or quality spaces is of any explanatory value whatsoever. People do catch on to the use

8. 'Linguistics and Philosophy' in *Language and Philosophy*, ed. S. Hook (New York: New York University Press, 1970), p. 96.

of the word 'green' by groping and exploring the words and the world. That is puzzling, but puzzlement, urges Goodman, ought not to be buried in an empty mystique of innateness.

Recent interest in the underdetermined character of experience comes neither from Geach nor grue. It owes its vogue to Noam Chomsky. His first target has been not the learning of words but the mastery of grammar. Early in life children learn to speak grammatically. The actual collection of things said in a child's presence completely underdetermines the grammar of English. The child is soon able to utter not only what it has overheard, but a lot of new sentences never uttered by anyone before. A vast horde of 'possible grammars' are compatible with what is actually said in front of the child but with little hesitation children of suitable age project the 'right' grammar on the basis of what they hear. So Chomsky proposes that children are born with an innate ability to make the right projection.

Virtually any child will pick up the language of any community in which it finds itself. Rather than postulate that every child is born with a hundred innate grammars (Japanese, Chicano, Kwakiutl, and French) it is a better guess that all languages share a single underlying structure, and that children are born with a disposition to follow this structure in projecting an actual language on the basis of what is said around them.

Aside from the word 'innate' we may seem to have come some distance from Descartes. Quite the contrary: Noam Chomsky has pointed the parallels with great skill.[9] Chief among them is a view of what is distinctive about human beings. Descartes contributed much to our mechanistic view of the world – the view that all phenomena are to be explained mechanically (or by latter-day electrochemistry or whatever). Many of his contemporaries and successors favoured this view of man as well. Descartes thought he could

9. *Cartesian Linguistics: A Chapter in the History of Rationalist Thought* (New York: Harper and Row, 1966).

find a mechanical explanation for all human action except speech. In a passage in his *Discourse on Method* that Chomsky also quotes, Descartes says he can regard the *body* as a machine except that,

if there were machines which bore a resemblance to our body and imitated our actions as far as it was morally possible to do so, we should always have two very certain tests by which to recognise that, for all that, they were not real men. The first is, that they could never use speech or other signs as we do when placing our thoughts on record for the benefit of others. For we can easily understand a machine's being constituted so that it can utter words, and even emit some responses to action on it of a corporeal kind . . . But it never happens that it arranges its speech in various ways, in order to reply appropriately to everything that may be said in its presence, as even the lowest type of man can do. (*Discourse*, Part V)

Chomsky sums up this position by saying that 'man has a species-specific capacity, a unique type of intellectual organization which cannot be attributed to peripheral organs or related to general intelligence and which manifests itself in what we may refer to as the "creative aspect" of language use' (*Cartesian Linguistics*, pp. 4–5).

Part of Chomsky's conjectured explication of the capacity that Descartes thought peculiar to the human species is a species-specific innate human grammar. This speculation does appear open in the long run to observational verification or refutation. It is not a matter of 'looking to see' whether all languages have 'something in common'. What is required is a theory of grammar enabling us to see what is essential to the structure of languages. The catchword 'innate' is the signal for a new research programme in linguistics. Before Chomsky, linguists thought their job was to describe each language in its own right. Only given a description of a particular language, say Sanskrit, could one ask how people actually learn the independent entity that has been described. After Chomsky, the task is reversed. One should not try to describe each individual language as an independent entity, but strive for descriptions of a structure explaining how a child can learn it and any other human language. Explanations must be determined by what can theoretically be attributed to a child. The more one thinks the child brings to the language, the more one will be influenced by innatism in constructing models of the grammars of languages.

Many old speculations gain new life in this hypothetico-experimental setting. We once speculated about a child born into an alien universe. Would it, as the rationalist implies, still have the concept of mother, even though its new environment never elicits it? To attribute innate concepts must be to attribute a theoretical structure that can explain how infants enter our intellectual world. If the only structures proposed and surviving experimental test imply that humans are electro-chemically disposed always to react to mother-features, then we can abruptly say that motherhood is innate. But if we are like chicks that can be 'imprinted' on to buffalo or scholars and subsequently disdain the company of fowl, then imprinting is native but motherhood is not. The television version of the child in the alien universe is the child confronting extra-galactic aliens. On Chomsky's view, the ability to acquire human language is innate, and has evolved over one or nine million years of human history. Transport your infant to the Indies, ensure that it will be succoured, and it will grow up a native speaker. But transport it to a planet whose life, however humanoid, has a different evolutionary past, and so is a different species: then your child will not be able to infer the grammar of that alien language from the speech around it. Maybe cunning linguists already speaking human will do it, much as after decades of work they 'crack genetic codes' that determine human inheritance. But human infants could not catch on in Arcturus as they can in the Arctic.

This speculation is not a description of an experiment but a moral to be drawn from universal grammar, if it exists. The very characteristics of humans that explain how children learn any human language could only by cosmic accident help in learning an extra-terrestrial lingo. The task now is to state these characteristics with some precision. Work goes on apace, although not always with much success: a point to which we shall return.

The work goes on with such enthusiasm that other aspects of the old story about innate ideas get forgotten. Take for example the problem of mathematical truth. Wittgenstein, in his unfinished *Remarks on the Foundations of Mathematics*, was, concurrently but independently of Goodman, drawing attention to the underdetermined character of mathematical concepts. He went so far as to suggest that a mathematical theorem did not have the marks of necessity until it was proven. But he thought that once a proof was pointed out to us, we could not fail to accept it, except on pain of being called stupid or irrational. That which makes us accept proofs is not our training in mathematical skills and concepts but is a precondition for those skills and concepts, and lies in human nature. It is innate. To be human is to be able to prove a little. A man 'who will not reason about anything', is, as Aristotle says, 'no better than a vegetable' (*Metaphysics*, 1006a).

Clearly any philosopher who supposes, with Descartes and Chomsky, that man and beast are distinguished by the ability to speak, must suppose that language matters to philosophy. But the species-specific character of language is only an ingenious corollary of Chomsky's speculations. The central philosophical implication is that knowledge of the structure of human language will tell us something profound about the nature of the human mind. Parallel to this one may imagine another doctrine, that the structure of language is related to the nature of reality beyond the mind. This is the topic of our next chapter. Communication, meaning, Fregean *Sinn* seem a modest and proper object of academic enquiry. But it leads directly to something utterly immodest – although argued by our most careful and cogent thinkers – the doctrine that once we understand how meanings can be mastered and conveyed, we shall also have learned things of the greatest importance about the mind and the world.

7. Bertrand Russell's acquaintance

The influence of language on philosophy has, I believe, been profound and almost unrecognized. If we are not to be misled by this influence, it is necessary to become conscious of it, and to ask ourselves deliberately how far it is legitimate. The subject–predicate logic, with the substance–attribute metaphysic, are a case in point. It is doubtful whether either would have been invented by people speaking a non-Aryan language; certainly they do not seem to have arisen in China, except in connection with Buddhism, which brought Indian philosophy with it. Again, it is natural, to take a different kind of instance, to suppose that a proper name which can be used significantly stands for a single entity; we suppose that there is a certain more or less persistent being called 'Socrates', because the same name is applied to a series of occurrences which we are led to regard as appearances of this one being.[1]

It is curious how often, in various generations, a philosopher has said that the influence of language on philosophy has been profound and almost unrecognized. Perhaps the reason for the iteration of this theme is that different generations discover their own linguistic influences. Russell is a case in point. This chapter will describe a remarkable metaphysical scheme, most of which evolved rather late in his philosophical career. We shall note how much of it is couched in terms of language. It is not the best example of Russell's work, but it

1. Bertrand Russell, 'Logical Atomism' (1924), reprinted in *Logic and Knowledge*, ed. R. Marsh (London: Allen and Unwin, 1956), pp. 330-1. This anthology is hereafter cited as *LK*.

does follow from some of his most important contributions to philosophy, and it serves to introduce themes that will occupy us in later chapters.

Just as Russell's work in logic was, to begin with, driven by a desire to understand the foundations of mathematics, so the epistemology tries to understand the nature of knowledge which, it is assumed, must ultimately be derived from the senses. In the case of mathematics despite what Russell occasionally said in unreflective moments, the aim was not to shore up standard mathematics but to understand why it needed no support. Contrary to much folklore, the 'foundations' provided by axioms were not certain and only conjectured.

In mathematics, the greatest degree of self-evidence is usually not to be found quite at the beginning, but at some later point; hence the early deductions, until they reach this point, give reasons rather for believing the premises because true consequences follow from them, than for believing the consequences because they follow from the premises.[2]

Similarly the aim of Russell's epistemology was not so much to refute scepticism by providing infallible axioms, as to offer a speculative theory that would explain why scepticism is absurd. We shall not go direct into Russell's epistemology — the reader may consult Pears for that — but proceed at once with a linguistic bent.

Although Russell is concerned with many of the problems of Berkeley or Locke, he learned from G. E. Moore categorically to reject the theory of ideas. In a 1914 paper, 'On the nature of Acquaintance', there is a mature statement of his opposition to 'the theory that the immediate object is mental, as well as the subject' (*LK*, p. 127). This rules out the possibility of, or at least any motive for, an ideational theory of meaning. Meaning, for Russell, does have to do with immedi-

---

2. A. N. Whitehead and B. Russell, *Principia Mathematica* (Cambridge: University Press, 1910), I, p. v.

ate objects, but since these are not seventeenth-century 'ideas', meaning does not have to do with ideas. The question then arises as to what the 'immediate objects' are. Here we find a remarkable development in Russell's thought lasting two or three decades. A seemingly straightforward epistemology is dragged by logic and a theory of meaning into one of the most exotic metaphysics yet presented. We call it 'logical atomism'.

In the beginning Russell thought that the things with which I am acquainted are the immediate objects of experience. He was acquainted with Stalin, and Stalin was, briefly, an immediate object for Russell; so was his own pipe. If, at a party, someone said, 'Stalin looks sober but really he must be drunk', and was asked, 'Who do you mean?' an appropriate reply is pointing, perhaps saying also, 'The man who is now grinning at Roosevelt.' What is the meaning of the name 'Stalin'? This fragment of discourse suggests that it is the very man Stalin that is meant.

Frege, it will be recalled, had three categories: reference, sense, and associated idea. He and Russell agreed in discounting the third. Frege thought that the reference of the name 'Stalin' would be the very man Stalin. This name also had a sense, a public meaning which makes it possible for successive generations of historians to refer to the Soviet leader. Here Russell differs from Frege. He rejects 'senses', *Sinn*, or public meanings other than reference. He argues against Frege, rather unclearly, in the famous 1905 paper 'On Denoting'.[3] Whatever the merits of the arguments, Russell unequivocally opts for what Alston calls a referential theory of meaning. See Chapter 2 above: according to a referential theory, the meaning of an expression is that to which we refer when using the expression.

3. In *LK*. Russell stated better anti-Fregean arguments in 1911: 'Knowledge by Acquaintance and Knowledge by Description', reprinted in his *Mysticism and Logic* (Harmondsworth: Penguin, 1953, pp. 197-218.

If I say, 'The marigold over there is orange', and there is a unique marigold over there, then, according to a referential theory, that very marigold would be a good candidate for the meaning of 'the marigold over there.' That flower is what the phrase, on this occasion of utterance, actually denotes. What about 'orange' or 'is orange'? Russell was inclined to say that this denotes an abstract universal, orangeness, with which I have been directly acquainted. Many philosophers, from Aristotle on, have doubted that there was any abstract universal to be acquainted with. Such an entity as a universal will certainly be news to most laymen. Russell was unmoved.

Seeing that nearly all the words to be found in the dictionary stand for universals, it is strange that hardly anybody except students of philosophy ever realizes that there are such entities as universals.[4]

Russell did not believe that every abstract word stands for a universal. Some do, while other abstractions are to be analysed in terms of simple abstractions which ultimately stand for universals.

Universals may serve as the reference of predicates, but subjects can create more problems. 'The golden mountain does not exist.' This statement is meaningful and indeed true. Hence 'the golden mountain' must be meaningful, yet there is no golden mountain for it to refer to. Russell first thought that 'the golden mountain' might refer to a strange quasimental object which has independent 'being', and which 'subsists' although it does not exist. In 1903 he wrote:

Being is that which belongs to every conceivable term, to every possible object of thought – in short to everything that can possibly occur in any proposition, true or false, and to all such propositions themselves. Being belongs to whatever can be counted . . . Numbers, the Homeric gods, relations, chimeras and four-dimensional spaces all have being, for if they were not entities of a kind, we could make no propositions about them. Thus being is a

4. *The Problems of Philosophy* (London: Home University Library, 1911), pp. 93-4.

general attribute of everything, and to mention anything is to show that it is. *Existence*, on the contrary, is the prerogative of some only amongst beings.[5]

Two years later in 'On Denoting' he was very rude indeed about anyone who could hold such a doctrine!

'Something is a golden mountain' contains no reference to the golden mountain, although it does refer to universals of goldness and mountainhood, which do exist. Equally, 'It is not the case that something is a golden mountain' does not refer to the golden mountain, and yet means roughly the same as the misleading 'the golden mountain does not exist'. Russell concluded that the latter sentence only seems to be in subject–predicate form; perhaps its grammatical form is subject–predicate, but its logical form is 'It is not the case that something is a golden mountain.' Similar devices enable us to paraphrase other troublesome cases. 'The present king of France is bald' is perfectly meaningful. But the meaning of 'the present king of France' cannot be a person, for there is no king of France. Instead we paraphrase the sentence, in subject – predicate form, into a more complex sentence: 'There is one and only one present king of France, and every present king of France is bald.' This sentence is commendably false, and all of its components are meaningful. 'Meaningful', for Russell, means, remember, 'stands for', or, 'has reference'.

'The present king of France' is a description which, if uttered seriously on some occasion, may purport to denote a definite individual. The same is true of 'the marigold over there', which, at the time and place that I write these words, really does denote one definite flower. Expressions of the form 'the *F*' are called definite descriptions. For simplicity they should have parallel analyses. The example about the king of France shows that 'the *F*' does not necessarily refer to

5. *The Principles of Mathematics* (London: Allen and Unwin, 1903), p. 449.

anything. We get over that difficulty by translating sentences of the form 'The *F* is *G*' as 'One and only one thing is *F*, and everything that is *F* is *G*.' In this theory of definite descriptions, the denoting phrase 'the *F*' occurs as grammatical subject, but because it requires this analysis it cannot be what Russell calls a 'logical subject'. That is, it is not the subject of the sentence given by logical analysis. The analysed sentence has no simple subject.

Next, take Stalin. Russell, at least briefly, could say, 'I don't trust Stalin', and be referring to a man who was his immediate object of acquaintance. But if today I say, 'Stalin became an ogre', I am referring to the same man, but there is no immediate object of *my* experience to whom I am referring. For a referential theory of meaning, as such, this is no problem; 'Stalin', we could say, means just the same man in my utterance as in Russell's. That is, it means the man it denotes. But now Russell's empiricist epistemology intrudes. The meaning of all our terms is acquired by experience. According to Russell that implies that a correct analysis of the meaning will involve the experiences from which the meaning was acquired. What Russell means by 'Stalin' is the very man with whom he was acquainted. Not having had that privilege, what I mean by 'Stalin' is, perhaps 'the despot who ruled the Soviet Union during the early years of my life', or 'the man chiefly responsible for transforming Leninism into tyranny', or some such. This procedure has a remarkable consequence. My friend, perhaps, means by 'Stalin' 'the man whose selfless leadership prevented the destruction of Moscow'. Although we are perfectly able to communicate about Stalin, we do not mean that same thing by our words! This did not disturb Russell:

When one person uses a word, he does not mean by it the same thing as another person means by it. I have often heard it said that that is a misfortune. This is a mistake. It would be absolutely fatal if people meant the same things by their words. It would make all intercourse impossible, and language the most hopeless and useless thing imaginable, because the meaning you attach to your words must depend on the nature of the objects you are acquainted with, and since different people are acquainted with different objects, they would not be able to talk to each other unless they attached quite different meanings to their words. We should have to talk only about logic – a not wholly undesirable result. Take, for example, the word 'Piccadilly'. We, who are acquainted with Piccadilly, attach quite a different meaning to that word from any which could be attached to it by a person who had never been in London: and, supposing that you travel in foreign parts and expatiate on Piccadilly, you will convey to your hearers entirely different propositions from those in your mind . . . If you were to insist on language which was unambiguous, you would be unable to tell people at home what you had seen in foreign parts. It would be altogether incredibly inconvenient to have an unambiguous language, and therefore mercifully we have not got one. (*LK*, pp. 195–6)

As a corollary, 'A logically perfect language, if it could be constructed, would not only be intolerably prolix, but, as regards its vocabulary, would be very largely private to one speaker' (p. 198).

A theory of meaning, I said, is about what is public in language, about what makes communication possible; it concerns that for which Frege postulated an objective public somewhat that he called the 'sense' of our words. Russell rejected Frege and opted for a referential theory of meaning. His epistemology leads to the conclusion that meaning is essentially private. According to his theory of meaning, communication occurs only thanks to the good luck of ambiguity.

Unreflectively one might have expected a theorist of ideas to favour the notion of a private language, while the referentialist deals with public languages. After all, what we refer to is typically public, whereas 'ideas' are ineluctably private. But quite the reverse situation comes to light. Because of his epistemology, the arch-referentialist Russell urges that meaning is private and that communication occurs only through ambiguity, whereas Locke acknowledges (though he has no interest in a theory about) the common acceptation of terms which is shared by the public.

The extent of the privacy of Russell's language depends on the epistemology. We are to be allowed to refer, without need of analysis, only to 'immediate objects'. These are referred to by names, real names, 'logically proper names', which he described as follows:

At any given moment, there are certain things of which a man is 'aware', certain things which are 'before his mind'. Now although it is very difficult to define 'awareness', it is not at all difficult to say that I am aware of such and such things. If I am asked, I can reply that I am aware of this, and that, and the other, and so on through a heterogeneous collection of objects. If I describe these objects, I may of course describe them wrongly; hence I cannot with certainty communicate to another what are the things of which I am aware. But if I speak to myself, and denote them by what may be called 'proper names', rather than by descriptive words, I cannot be in error. (*LK*, p. 130)

When I speak to myself using logically proper names, 'I cannot be in error', says Russell. Remember Berkeley, as quoted in Chapter 4 above: 'So long as I confine my thoughts to my own ideas, divested of words, I do not see how I can easily be mistaken.' Russell ended almost at Berkeley's position although he began by violent opposition to it. The trouble arises over the elements of which we are 'directly aware'. In the early days of the theory one could be directly aware of Stalin or Russell's pipe. But Russell's pipe is an ongoing temporal object, once part of a briar tree and now perhaps reverently installed in a museum in Ontario. As the theory evolved Russell began to claim that he was not immediately aware of *that* object. To illustrate the point, Russell held up a piece of chalk, saying 'This is white . . . I do not want you to think about the piece of chalk I am holding, but of what you see when you look at the chalk' (p. 198). 'This', used as a name, does not denote the chalk, as it does in common speech, but something like the sense-datum of the chalk.

It is fortunate that the word 'this' can be used as a proper name, for

it is very difficult to get any instance of a name at all in the proper strict logical sense of the word. The only words one does use as names in the logical sense are words like 'this' or 'that'. One can use 'this' as a name to stand for a particular with which one is acquainted at the moment. We say 'This is white'. If you agree that 'This is white', meaning the 'this' that you see, you are using 'this' as a proper name. But if you try to apprehend the proposition that I am expressing when I say 'This is white', you cannot do it. If you mean this piece of chalk as a physical object, then you are not using a proper name. It is only when you use 'this' quite strictly, to stand for an actual object of sense, that it is really a proper name. And in that it has a very odd property for a proper name, namely that it seldom means the same thing two moments running and does not mean the same thing to the speaker and to the hearer. It is an *ambiguous* proper name, but it is really a proper name all the same, and it is almost the only thing I can think of that is used properly and logically in the sense that I was talking of for a proper name. (p. 201)

An astute questioner asked, 'If the proper name of a thing, a "this" varies from instant to instant, how is it possible to make any argument?' It took Bertrand Russell to reply:

You can keep 'this' going for about a minute or two. I made that dot and talked about it for some little time. I mean it varies often. If you argue quickly, you can get some little way before it is finished. I think things last for a finite time, a matter of some seconds or minutes or whatever it may happen to be. (p. 203)

Speculations such as these show what Russell meant in the long quotation with which I began this chapter. He thought that language makes us 'suppose that a proper name can be used significantly to stand for a single entity; we suppose that there is a certain more or less persistent thing called 'Socrates' because the same name is applied to a series of occurrences which we are led to regard as appearances of this one being'. A new theory about language is intended to convince us that there is no such entity that we know about; Socrates, Stalin, Russell's pipe, and your left thumb are logical constructions out of entities (denoted by various utterances of the word 'this') that we do know about.

It cannot be too strongly emphasized that the referential

theory of meaning, which I have attributed to Russell, is not entirely responsible for the remarkable metaphysics of logical atomism. Russell's theory of language acquisition, which derives from his increasingly extreme empiricism, is what forces him along this road. He supposes that meaningful expressions mean what they denote, and that you can know what an expression means only if you are acquainted, by actual experience, with what is denoted. Hence very few expressions have meaning. Most descriptions and names are what Russell called incomplete expressions, and the sentences in which they occur must be analysed into sentences in which they do not occur. It is perfectly possible to hold a referential theory of meaning for ordinary proper names, like 'Stalin', claiming that they simply denote and have no Fregean sense at all.[6]

Russell did not actively maintain his logical atomism for very long. He wrote a good deal of philosophy after 1924, but little of it was in this vein. It is possible to hold that much of the work published between 1912 and 1924 was a consequence of the bad influence that Wittgenstein exerted on him. Although Russell's doctrines appear to be entirely different from those of Wittgenstein's *Tractatus*, it is as if Russell felt bound to make his theory of language and epistemology follow a road traced out by the *Tractatus*. This was a disaster, because the *Tractatus* is not concerned with epistemology at all, and Russell's radical theory of language acquisition, in that alien environment, drove him to the extremes that we have quoted.

This diagnosis is not necessarily right. Perhaps P. F. Strawson's book *Individuals* provides us with the best-developed body of doctrines that are explicitly contrary to those held by Russell. He argues that it is impossible to have any language in which one is able to say the sorts of things that we do say,

---

6. Saul Kripke, 'Naming and Necessity', in *Semantics of Natural Languages*, ed. D. Davidson and G. Harman (Dordrecht: Reidel, 1972).

without taking for granted the existence of bodies both material and human. Russell's analysing away Stalin and pipes is in principle impossible. Just as Russell warned us of the influence of language on philosophy, so Strawson inveighs against the disastrous effect of Russell's theory about language. It all starts, Strawson has argued, from Russell's mistaken referential theory of meaning. Certainly there is some truth in this; had Russell accepted Frege's notion of sense as opposed to reference as a concept of meaning, he would have found it far less natural to combine his theory of knowledge with his theory of language to produce his remarkable metaphysics. Yet the theory of language acquisition seems to me just as important.

Not everything in Russell hinges on the referential theory and language acquisition. Our opening quotation mentions the 'subject–predicate logic, with the substance–attribute metaphysic', both distasteful to Russell, and both, he thought, superseded. Our grammars commonly analyse sentences into subject-predicate form. The subject appears to stand for something which has predicates. Hence (thought Russell) arises an ontology of substances (for which subjects stand) possessing attributes (designated by predicates). It is a strange ontology, for the substance becomes a sort of in-cushion into which the pins of attributes are stuck. The substance, before having any attributes pinned to it, seems to be what Locke long ago ironically called an 'I know not what'. This is an altogether too simple view of the theory of substance, which arises from a host of related philosophical doctrines. Notice, however, how the theory of descriptions, eliminating many subjects in favour of sentences built up from quantifiers ('there exists', and 'all') shows us how to talk about the world without postulating substances for which subjects stand. The grammatical subject is eliminated. This point of view has been carried further in the work of W.v.O. Quine. In his book *Word and Object* he urges a 'canonical language' freed, by techniques like the theory of descriptions, from any referring expressions, and hence from any drive to postulate substances. This does not prove that a theory of substances is wrong, but Russell has some plausibility when he says that neither subject–predicate logic nor substance–attribute metaphysic would have been invented by people not speaking a language like ours. There is a firm suggestion that both the logic and the metaphysic are artefacts of language, not reality.

The substance–attribute question and the question as to whether we know of entities like Stalin are closely related. Strawson is as firmly opposed to Russell on the one question as the other. The first part of *Individuals* defends substances (of a sort) and the second defends the old grammar. In particular it argues that one simply could not learn, as one's first language, a 'canonical language' in the spirit of Russell and Quine; we can master those languages only because we already know an 'ordinary' language that enables us to refer directly to particular enduring things.

Such questions are both of current interest and of lasting importance. One way in which we could develop them here would be to give some account of Strawson's own theories about language and their relation to his epistemology. There is an alternative, which is to take seriously Russell's claim that he has found the 'logical form' of the things we say, that underlies their superficial 'grammatical form'. We shall take this up in the next chapter and connect it with the work of linguists, both of the seventeenth century and of the present. In the end it will lead us to the same family of problems about the substance–attribute distinction and yet give us a new and potentially very effective means of solution.

8. Ludwig Wittgenstein's articulation

Russell was convinced that he had discovered that logical form differs from grammatical form. 'The king of France is bald' is a sentence whose grammatical form appears to be: [Subject (The king of France)] + [Predicate (is bald)]. But the logical form is a conjunction of three sentences, none of which is in subject–predicate form: there is at least one king of France, there is at most one, and every king of France is bald. This notion of logical form needs a good deal of elucidation.

A deductive argument is called *valid* if the conclusion follows from the premises. (This is a technical use of the term 'valid'. In common speech, a valid argument is often simply a persuasive argument. An argument can fail to be rationally persuasive for two distinct reasons: it may be invalid, or the premises may not all be known to be true. Validity, in the jargon of logicians, has to do with deductive consequence, not soundness of the premises.) It is commonly held that a deductive argument, if valid, is valid in virtue of its form, not its content. Thus, 'All my teachers are men, all men are mortal, so all my teachers are mortal' is not valid in virtue of anything about male teachers; validity has to do with the form 'all *A* are *B*, all *B* are *C*, so all *A* are *C*'. Logicians from Aristotle on have drawn up schemes of valid argument. An argument whose premises and conclusion have the forms of the steps in a valid argument scheme, it itself a valid argument. So one tends to think of the conclusion. 'All my teachers are mortal' as having the form indicated by the scheme of the conclusion, 'all *A* are *C*'.

On the other hand, a single sentence may serve as premise or conclusion for many a valid argument, and may fit several different formal patterns. If we think of the occurrence of the same sentence in several different arguments, we may consistently describe different aspects of its form on different occasions, and hence conclude that there is no such thing as *the* logical form. This point is made more polemically by Strawson:

It remains to mention some of the ways in which people have spoken misleadingly of logical form. One of the commonest of these is to talk of *'the* logical form' of a statement; as if a statement could never have more than one kind of formal power; as if statements could, in respect of their formal powers, be grouped in mutually exclusive classes, like animals at a zoo in respect of their species. But to say that a statement is of some one logical form is simply to point to a certain general class of, e.g., valid inferences, in which the statement can play a certain role. It is not to exclude the possibility of there being other general classes of valid inferences in which the statement can play a certain role.[1]

The most notable of these unnamed 'people' to whom Strawson refers, but does not name, must be Russell. Russell's claim to investigate *the* logical form of some sentences seems confuted by Strawson's observations only if we suppose that Russell was concerned solely with the power of sentences to occur in inferences. Russell is making a stronger claim. He asserts that any sentence has a certain feature, its logical form, which makes it possible for the sentence to have meaning in all those utterances where it does have meaning. This logical form has to do with projecting the conditions under which this sentence is true when uttered. Moreover, this logical form will be the underlying kernel of all of Strawson's log-

---

1. P. F. Strawson, *Introduction to Logical Theory* (London: Methuen; New York: Wiley, 1952), p. 53.

ical forms for a single sentence. It will predict just which forms of argument are such that the sentence in question has the power to serve as premise or conclusion.

Logicians were traditionally interested in inference, but let us take more seriously the other side of Russell's conception of a unique logical form: that it has something to do with the conditions under which a sentence is true. This leads us to a line of thought prominent in Wittgenstein's *Tractatus*. Truths, according to one popular theory of truth, somehow match up with facts. So we might expect the structure of a sentence expressing a truth to match the structure of the fact that it expresses. The structure of facts might then be investigated by discovering the logical form of true sentences that correspond to them. This swift train of thought invites us to do speculative metaphysics on the grand scale! Can we discover something fundamental about the possibilities of the world by investigating the logical form of our sentences? This may seem monstrous armchair philosophy. Surely we cannot find out about the world by linguistic or logical analysis. But of course such analysis would teach us only the *possible* forms of facts, not the actual facts. We might learn that *if F* is a fact, it has such and such a form, but not that *F* is a fact. Moreover there is in the *Tractatus* (though not, I think, in Russell) an element of what we might call 'linguistic idealism'. That is, the structure of possible facts, and hence of the world with which I am acquainted, is bounded by my language. '*The limits of my language* mean the limits of my world' (5.6). 'The world is *my* world: this is manifest in the fact that the limits of *language* (of that language which alone I understand) mean the limits of *my* world' (5.62). The realist angrily says that the world is there, language or no. The idealist Berkeley says that to be is to be perceived; there is no world other than the perceived one. The extreme linguistic idealist would say, to be is to be spoken about; there is no world there except what is spoken about. A milder doctrine is not altogether foreign to the *Tractatus*: to be capable of being is to be capable of being spoken about. The world is autonomous, but the possibilities of the world are not; the world plays out its own life, but only on the 'logical scaffolding' of my language.

We shall have occasion to think more about 'linguistic idealism', but not now. Russell had no part in it. Suffice it to say that in the concept of logical form Russell was after far bigger things than the power of sentences to occur in this or that valid argument. To understand part of what Russell and Wittgenstein were doing, I shall first step backwards in time and then forwards. Forwards to the present, but first backwards to the seventeenth century once again.

The students of Port Royal produced not only the classic logic book but also the classic grammar, and they deemed the latter a more fundamental contribution than their logic. Port Royal was part of a widespread industry of writing grammar books. Grammar, which before and after was a torment for schoolboys and the intricate delight of a few scholars, was, for a while, a central preoccupation of intellectuals. In particular there sprang up a whole series of investigations into so-called general or universal grammar. Chomsky's little book *Cartesian Linguistics* is a lively guide to some of these trends, although it is strongly and avowedly coloured by his own concerns which we shall soon discuss. Chapter 4 of Michel Foucault's *The Order of Things* is a dense source of information that illustrates other aspects of this enterprise. In particular, Chomsky takes 'universal grammar' to mean a single grammar that underlies every human tongue. Foucault in contrast reminds us that instead there evolved the idea of a universal grammar of each particular language, not necessarily pertaining to any other language. An instructive pointer in this direction is the very title of a book published by Claude Buffier in 1704: *The Elements of Metaphysics, or, French Grammar According to a New Plan*. The grammar of ordinary French was a way of doing metaphysics.

The central metaphysical problem of the time inevitably derived from the doctrine of ideas, but it is not peculiar to ideas. We can begin to see a problem on contemplating the trio: ideas, words, things. Things are wholes, but words are articulated. The marigold is at once a brilliant orange, two inches across, and has eleven petals. But our assertions about it come in little articulated bits: 'the marigold is orange and it has eleven petals'. As for our idea of the marigold, it is unclear whether it is articulated or not. Berkeley thought not; indeed that is a chief part of his assault on abstract ideas. There is no abstract idea of 'orange.' There are only ideas of this marigold or that tangerine, each with its own individual nature. There is no articulation of the marigold into colour There is no abstract idea of 'orange'. There are only ideas of abstract ideas thought that ideas could be articulated: we can contemplate orangencss and we can contemplate flowerhood. But regardless of the variant theories of ideas, how does representation in words (of either idea or of things) actually work, when the words come out in a string and the marigold does not? The most naturally occurring analysis concerns sentences of subject–predicate form: 'The marigold is orange.' Draw up a square like this:

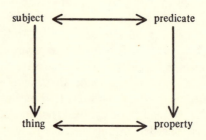

We assert that *S* is *P*. *S* refers to a thing; reference goes down the left side of the square. *P* indicates a property; this goes down the right side of the square. If these two downward strokes succeed, and we successfully refer to a thing and indicate a property, then we can start saying something. We assert *S* is *P*. Assertion proceeds across the top of the square. The assertion is true if the thing referred to has the property indicated by the *S* and *P* that are copulated. If the world fills in the bottom horizontal line, it presents us with a fact.

Here then we have a fine scheme on which to found a theory of reference, properties, facts, truth, and meaning. Unfortunately when we actually look at an object it is not so clear that we see a thing, on the one hand, and a property on the other. What we see is more like this, except in colour:

The problem of general grammar is to explain how articulated language effects the representation of a non-articulated part of the world. If we are faithful to our experience, we have to replace our square by a triangle:

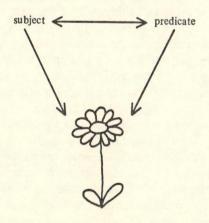

This diagram is much more mysterious, and raises two problems, first, how do the two downward arrows work in different ways, and secondly – the pressing problem for our general grammarians – what is the nature of the copula which rejoins what is separate?

There was no *a priori* reason for thinking that every language must make the copula work in the same way, so one might have different general grammars for different families of language. In the seventeenth century there remained vestiges of an historical view that led to the conjecture of a single universal grammar. There was supposed to be a single language before Babel. All post-Babel language would share some features of that. Moreover, Hebrew would be the language closest to pre-Babel. Hence a good many scholars tried to construct a universal grammar out of Hebrew and tried to make it fit Greek or French. Since this did not work very well, increasingly many workers turned, like Buffier, to the 'philosophical grammar' (as they sometimes called it) of particular languages. Hence arose general or universal grammars of *French*.

The second line of the *Tractatus* is a splendid one-sentence answer to the problems of articulation: 'The world is the totality of facts, not of things.' Both our marigold diagrams are wrong because they assume that the reality, to which our words must conform, is the essentially thingy marigold. On the contrary, the world is not made up of marigolds and Trafalgar Square and string and mosquitoes and rainbows. It is made up of facts. Facts moreover are articulated, and the sentence that represents the fact is of its nature articulated (3.141). Indeed it is 'only insofar as a proposition is logically segmented that it is a picture of a situation' (4.032). Just as it is asserted that 'An elementary proposition consists of names. It is a nexus, a concatenation, of names' (4.22), so it is said of the state of affairs, represented by the proposition 'objects fit into one another like the links in a chain'.

Scholars are never going to agree on what Wittgenstein's

'objects' are. They are not physical things, marigolds and curtain rods. Russell probably thought Wittgenstein's objects were sense data like the look of the chalk mentioned in the preceding chapter. That is certainly wrong, for *Tractatus* objects are as permanent as a language. The question of exactly what they are will keep the *Tractatus* industry going for a long time. I shall not add my speculations here. Suffice it to say that in part Wittgenstein is solving the old problem of general grammar by introducing a new way of understanding the world. The problem of general grammar is seen as unsolvable for a thingy world, so, since we do succeed in speaking truly, the world cannot be a collection of things, but of facts which already have the necessary articulation. Facts, moreover, are not to be seen as composed of things with properties, but as a nexus of 'objects'. The analysed proposition is not subject and predicate, but a concatenation of names.

The theory of descriptions, and Wittgenstein's association with Russell at the crucial period, were essential for abandoning the subject–predicate model. Wittgenstein went further than anyone else in trying to create a new model, and thereby remoulded his world. Despite the immense effect that Wittgenstein had on Russell, the latter did not take this part of the *Tractatus* very seriously. Indeed I do not think Russell ever believed the world is made up of facts, not things. You recall his example: 'this is white'. Something, possibly a sense datum, is referred to by the logically proper name 'this'. The thing referred to is said to have the quality of being white; we seem returned to the square diagram above. Russell's world is made up of particulars possessing universals and he tried to find out what the particulars are.

Russell's distinction between logical and grammatical form may be misleading. Perhaps logical form just is deep grammatical form. His logical form is in part an attempt to solve what, in an earlier era, would have been called the fundamental problem of grammar. Moreover, it is also an attempt to solve a problem of what, in the past decade or so, has once again come to be called grammar. Here we must step away from the old grammarians and consider the new ones, of whom the most notable is Noam Chomsky. What is a grammar? In Chomsky's early published work he says that a grammar is an algorithm for distinguishing grammatical sentences from ungrammatical ones. It is a set of rules that can be mechanically applied to a string of words to determine if, or to what extent, the string is a grammatical sentence. Any natural language is potentially infinite; there is no limit to the number of grammatical sentences. If there were, we could list them all, and our algorithm would be tedious but simple: see if the string of words in fact occurs in the list. But there is no upper bound on sentences of English. People can recognize all sorts of sentences as grammatical although no one has ever uttered them before.

A grammar ought to be more, indeed, than an algorithm. It should also be a model of whatever it is that enables people to recognize new grammatical sentences. The most natural model would use some system of generation, in which it was clear how new sentences were projected from a relatively simple base. On Chomsky's view this model is best provided by a distinction between 'surface structure' and 'deep structure'. The surface structure is represented by the actual sentences we utter and write. The deep structure underlying this is a set of simple kernel structures and rules for projecting these so as to generate the surface structure. In later work Chomsky urges a more encyclopedic kind of grammar which consists of two kinds of mappings. First there is depth grammar, mapped on to surface grammar as above. Then the surface grammar is itself mapped on to a 'reading' which is the common acceptation of the sentence when actually uttered. Thus grammar becomes part of a theory about how we understand what is said.

In our discussion of innate ideas we have already noticed a further corollary that Chomsky draws from this programme.

The system of projections just described is specific and complex. A great many such systems would fit the actual speech overheard by an infant. Yet very quickly the infant picks on more or less the right system; that is, it learns to project in almost exactly the right way. Overheard speech 'underdetermines' (in the sense of Chapter 6) the grammar that the child has to acquire. Hence the child must have a grammatical structure innate in it. But a child born of English parents will learn the grammar of whatever speech milieu it grows up in. Hence it either comes with hundreds of innate grammars, spanning the world from the Falkland Islands to Murmansk or else all languages have a single underlying structure, which is innate to every human infant.

Russell's idea of logical form as opposed to grammatical form is strikingly like Chomsky's idea of depth grammar as opposed to surface grammar. Of course Russell's forms, which we now call first-order predicate logic, look not at all like Chomsky's kernel. But it is not monstrous to propose that first-order predicate logic is the core of a deep grammar of English. Many a logic course for beginners teaches projection rules for transforming sentences of familiar English into a uniform underlying logical form. That is, they teach projection rules from deep structure (first-order logic) to surface grammar (English sentences). A foremost advocate of such a programme is Donald Davidson, whose theory of meaning and truth is the topic of Chapter 12.

Chomsky's followers think that Davidson's programme will not work well. By and large they hold that a sophisticated version of the subject–predicate structure is a good first guide to deep structure. Here we have a notable transformation in ancient problems about subject and predicate, substance and attribute. It is still an open question what the deep structure of English or any other language is. One answer, that of Russell and Davidson, leads to the view that the substance–attribute metaphysic is derived from a mistaken grammatical theory, which is strong, though not conclusive, reason for saying it is wrong. Another answer, that of followers of Chomsky, is that the basic, ancient, grammatical hunch was right. That can only help restore the substance–attribute metaphysics. Here is an example of an open question, which might be answered reasonably soon, and whose answer will certainly be taken to matter to philosophy. Chomsky has already asserted that the upshot will be a theory of the human mind. Suppose we were to say with Wittgenstein's *Tractatus* that the limits of language are the limits of the world. Then the logical–grammatical structures underlying our language would also be the forms of limit to our world.

9. *A. J. Ayer's verification*

To some extent it is possible to categorize important philosophical work as *speculative* or *critical*. Speculative philosophy tries to construct theories about reality, or the cosmos, or whatnot, in order to explain problematic features of what little we actually know about it. Thus Leibniz is one of the most speculative of philosophers. The word 'critical' comes from Kant's *Critique of Pure Reason.* Kant thought that Leibniz, among others, had endowed the universe with a good deal of structure which had been argued from inadequate, nay impossible, philosophical grounds. The speculative doctrines of monadology are not straightforwardly false, but are rather answers to a question which cannot have true or false answers. Leibniz vainly imagined (thought Kant) that reason can know the ultimate constituents of the universe. But no answer to the question 'What is the world ultimately composed of?' can be right. Kant elaborated his *Critique* partly in order to explain how such questions sound all right, while the very asking of them is a fundamental error.

Roughly speaking, speculative philosophy confronts a problem by constructing a theory that will solve the problem. Critical philosophy confronts a similar problem by showing that the problem is of a sort that cannot have an answer, and explains why we should have been misled into supposing that it has an answer. The distinction is crass, for of course Kant had a 'theory' to resolve the problems of philosophy, just as Leibniz did, but there is at least this much truth in the distinction: Kant's theory worked by ruling some questions out of order, whereas Leibniz wanted to answer every question that occurred to him.

Russell resembled Leibniz in several ways, including the speculative character of much of his philosophy. He wanted answers provided by quite general theories. In later life he had contempt for those who would dismiss difficulties as 'pseudo-problems'. Now that we have had a look at some speculative philosophy to which language has avowedly mattered, we should turn our attention to the critical side. Kant's *Critique of Pure Reason* is an analysis of the possibilities of and preconditions for knowledge. It is not, in any explicit way, much concerned with language, although recent commentators, such as P. F. Strawson and J. F. Bennett, have turned parts of the book into a treatise on meaning. The title of Strawson's commentary, *The Bounds of Sense*, appears to be a quadruple pun on the dual meanings of 'bound' and the dual meanings of 'sense', but the limits and excessive leaps that are chiefly discussed concern not the five senses but what it makes sense to say. This transformation of Kant's critical philosophy into a work on meaning is clearly significant. In this chapter, however, I shall present a critical philosophy which is more easily grasped than Kant's. Although it is in many ways as ambitious as Kant's, it is much less complex. Its key word is 'verification', and it originated in Vienna.

The philosophy club, commonly known as the Vienna Circle, that formed around Moritz Schlick in the 1920s has had an immense impact on philosophy subsequently written in English. This is partly because the Circle was so attuned to empiricist modes of thought traditionally attractive to Anglo-Saxon thinkers, and partly because National Socialism scattered the Circle around the English-speaking world, from New Zealand to California. In this chapter I shall focus on just one aspect of this influence, summed up by the famous verification principle. It was intended as a vigorous critical hammer to eliminate metaphysics, demolish pseudo-science, and transform ethics. It also had a wider effect, which some might call insidious, on the prevailing attitude to the study of many philosophical problems: philosophers who would never admit to accepting any verification principle still are found reasoning as if they did accept it. The success of the verification principle is amazing, for, as we shall see, no one has succeeded in stating it!

To express the matter less paradoxically, the fundamental tenet of empiricism is that all knowledge is derived from experience. The Vienna Circle added to this a doctrine about meaning. When does a speaker make an assertion about some matter of fact? Only, it was argued, when there is some relation between what he says and some experience which could bear on the truth of what he says. Variously formulated principles of verification have been tried out as exact statements of this relation, but all have failed. This is surprising, for on the face of it, it ought to be quite easy to express the intended empiricist relation between asserting a matter of fact and experiences bearing on the truth of that matter of fact.

In saying that no writer has succeeded in stating this relation, I mean that there are generally agreed desiderata for any such principle, and that all statements of the principle fail to meet these standards. Some sense of the standards may be found in Karl Popper's 1953 'Personal Report'.[1] Popper was never a member of the Circle, but he was in Vienna and despite his disagreement on substantive points was perplexed by the same problems and was in broad sympathy with the Circle's goals. These philosophers had a strong background in mathematics and the physical or social sciences, and were sure that the rigour of mathematical logic combined with the experimental method were the marks of sound epistemology. In this they were at odds with the ongoing intellectual excitement of Vienna at that time. In addition to extensive meta-

---

1. Reprinted as Chapter 1 in Karl Popper, *Conjectures and Refutations* (London: Routledge and Kegan Paul, 1963), pp. 33-65.

physical and theological speculation, there was much Marxist theorizing, while Freud's psychoanalysis seemed to many intellectuals to be one of the most promising of human inventions. Much of this ferment was presented as science. Indeed the German word for science, which has wider connotations than ours, must inevitably include these activities as science. This is embarrassing if one does not care for these activities and yet takes science, whose highest form is physics, as the paradigm of rational human activity and the only road to knowledge. So there arises what Popper calls the problem of demarcation, of sorting the good science from the bad or pseudo-science.

Popper's demarcation was not necessarily between lovable sheep and repulsive goats. On the contrary, he thought that prescientific speculation might be and often had been immensely bolder and more productive than mere routine scientific activity, and he thought that such 'metaphysics' might be encouraged as a prolegomenon to science. The Vienna Circle was more radical. Most of its members urged that meaning itself is the line of demarcation. Physics has meaning, metaphysics does not. Rudolf Carnap proclaimed that 'In the domain of *metaphysics*, including all philosophy of value and normative theory, logical analysis yields the negative result *that the alleged statements in this domain are entirely meaningless*. Therewith a radical elimination of metaphysics is attained.'[2] In afterthought, former members of the Circle qualified such pronouncements a little, saying that something called 'cognitive meaning' is in question. But the substance was not changed: declarative sentences that lack cognitive meaning cannot be used to *say* anything, make no assertion; at best they excite emotions or suggest novelties that they cannot actually express. As Schlick said, 'Metaphysics col-

2. 'The Elimination of Metaphysics through Logical Analysis of Language' (1932), trans. in *Logical Positivism*, ed. A. J. Ayer (New York: Free Press, 1959), pp. 60-1. This anthology is hereafter cited as *LP*.

lapses not because the solving of its tasks is an enterprise to which the human reason is unequal (as for example Kant thought) but because there is no such task.'[3]

Carnap was able to score rhetorical success by quoting passages from Martin Heidegger, concluding with the curious sentence 'The Nothing itself nothings' (*LP*, p. 69). After being taken out of context and then wrenched into English, that sounds meaningless on anyone's standards. Despite such bizarre examples, it proved hard to state any general criterion of meaningfulness that would eliminate all metaphysics at one swoop. We must not pay too much attention to Schlick's oft-quoted slogan 'The meaning of a proposition is its method of verification.'[4] That motto could be taken as a theory of what meanings are; but as Schlick makes clear on the next page, his concern is chiefly with a 'criterion of meaning', that is, a test for marking off the meaningful utterances.

The basic idea is that any genuine proposition is verifiable. It was admitted on all sides that many meaningful statements are not in fact verifiable. In the course of an enquiry we may reach the point of saying that one of eighty parallel condensers was defective and by a short-circuit caused the fire that recently destroyed a space module, but there is in fact no possible way to proceed further and find out which was responsible. Yet 'Condenser number 5 caused the fire' is clearly meaningful. So is the proposition that ants will inherit the earth after humanity is extinct. By 'verifiable' we cannot intend 'in fact verifiable' but 'verifiable in principle'. Something is verifiable in principle if it is logically possible to verify it. It is not logically impossible that after our race is extinct, another should arise to verify our prediction about ants; it is not logically impossible that the aerospace techni-

---

3. 'The Turning Point in Philosophy' (1930), in *LP*, p. 57.
4. 'Meaning and Verification', *The Philosophical Review*, xxxxvi (1936), 261. Reprinted in *Readings in Philosophical Analysis*, ed. H. Feigl and W. Sellars (New York: Appleton–Century Crofts, 1949), pp. 146-70.

cian who fitted condenser number 5 should tomorrow confess that he deliberately installed a defective component. 'Actually, in practice, verifiable' provides too stringent a criterion of meaningfulness. It excludes much that is meaningful to members of the Vienna Circle. So it is amended to 'verifiable in principle', or, 'verifiable in theory'.

Next, it is a question whether verifiable means 'completely established' or not. There was some inclination to accept this view, for the concept of being conclusively verified seemed, at the time, quite a clear concept. But it was very stringent, for no truly universal proposition, not even 'All men are mortal', can be conclusively verified, for not every instance, past, present, and future, can be examined, even in principle. Nor is this difficulty restricted to universal propositions. It arises even for statements about particular things, as Schlick himself noticed. 'Strictly speaking, the meaning of a proposition about physical objects would be exhausted only by an indefinitely large number of possible verifications' (*LP*, p. 91). It is not logically possible to complete an indefinitely large number of observations, for indefinitely large is something like potentially infinite. So if 'verifiable' means 'conclusively verifiable' we should certainly sacrifice universal propositions, which are usually thought to be the centre of the physical sciences, and we should also abandon ordinary claims made for chairs and dahlias.

'Verifiable', then, is to be expanded as 'verifiable in principle', but not as 'conclusively verifiable in principle'. A cynic, on consulting a dictionary, may observe that 'inconclusive verification' is virtually a contradiction in terms. Popper was led to turn verificationism topsy-turvy. It is not verifying that marks good science from pseudo-science, he claimed, but falsifying. Universal propositions and propositions about objects can be proven false: a single counter-example will do. Popper did not offer this as a criterion of meaning; indeed he considered the obsession with meaning to be one of the worst features of the verificationists. So let us not be sidetracked, but pursue attempts to state a verification principle. Successive editions of A. J. Ayer's *Language, Truth and Logic* provide the most instructive illustration.[5] This lucid book presented the essence of the Vienna programme to English readers. Instead of using a thousand nuances and qualifications to hedge his statement of the verification principle, Ayer tried to present it briefly, naked. The most critical commentary on those youthful statements is by Ayer himself, in his newly published book, *The Central Questions of Philosophy*. But although on all accounts Ayer's first principles could not stand up to critical scrutiny, we owe him an immense debt for setting out the principles for scrutiny. Had he not done that, people might still believe that a statable verification principle lurked in the offing. We now know that there is none.

In the first edition of *Language, Truth and Logic* the principle is cast in the following form:

Let us call a proposition which records an actual or possible observation an experiential proposition. Then we may say that it is the mark of a genuine factual proposition, not that it should be equivalent to an experiential proposition, or any finite number of experiential propositions, but simply that some experiential propositions can be deduced from it in conjunction with certain other premises without being deducible from those other premises alone. (2nd ed., pp. 38–9)

Remember how verifiability-in-fact and conclusive-verifiability turned out to be too restrictive, damning most science and indeed most factual statements as meaningless. Ayer's version goes to the opposite extreme. To take an example of Isaiah Berlin's, 'if I say,

This logical problem is bright green
I dislike all shades of green
Therefore, I dislike this problem,

I have uttered a valid syllogism whose major premise has sat-

---

5. *Language, Truth and Logic* (London: Gollancz, first edition 1936; second edition with an important new introduction 1946).

isfied [Ayer's] definition of weak verifiability as well as the rules of logic and grammar, yet it is plainly meaningless.'[6] We began with criteria that were too stringent, but in attempting to rectify them, we have generated criteria that are too generous.

Matters now become complicated; I include them here to support my bald assertion that no correct verification principle has ever been stated. Here is Ayer's next try:

I propose to say that a statement is directly verifiable if it is either itself an observation-statement, or is such that in conjunction with one or more observation-statements it entails at least one observation-statement which is not deducible from those other premises alone; and I propose to say that a statement is indirectly verifiable if it satisfies the following conditions: first, that in conjunction with certain other premises it entails one or more directly verifiable statements which are not deducible from these other premises alone; and secondly, that these other premises do not include any statement that is not either analytic, or directly verifiable, or capable of being independently established as indirectly verifiable. And I can now reformulate the principle of verification as requiring of a literally meaningful statement, which is not analytic, that it should be either directly or indirectly verifiable, in the foregoing sense. (Introduction to 2nd ed., p. 13)

Alonzo Church sunk this with an ingenious example proving that Ayer's revised criterion is once again too liberal: any statement whatsoever is such that it is verifiable, and hence meaningful, or its negation is weakly verifiable, and hence meaningful. So at least one of 'The Nothing itself nothings' and 'The Nothing itself does not nothing' is meaningful. The argument is as follows.

Let N be for example Heidegger's 'nonsense-statement'.

6. 'Verification', *Proceedings of the Aristotelian Society*, XXXVIII (1938), 22. In general, for any nonsensical statement N and unrelated observation statement O, N follows from O and 'if N then O' so, on Ayer's first criterion, the nonsensical N must after all be 'meaningful'.

Take any three logically independent observation statements, O_1, O_2, O_3. Then the compound statement, call it C:

(not-O_1 and O_2) or (O_3 and not-N)

is certainly verifiable, because C, taken together with O_1, entails O_3. But C taken together with N entails O_2. Hence on Ayer's definition, N must be verifiable, *unless* N entails O_2 on its own. But looking back at C, we notice that this can happen only if O_3 and not-N jointly entail O_2. Since O_3 and O_2 are logically independent, it follows, on Ayer's criterion, that not-N is directly verifiable.[7]

This seems to have been the death-knell for attempts to characterize verifiability in terms of deducibility relations and observation statements. More details of this demise are given in a survey by C. G. Hempel.[8] He proposed that we should deliberately construct an 'empirically pure' language, all of whose descriptive terms are firmly linked with experience, and whose very grammar prevents our forming sentences that are not what we immediately recognize as testable. Then we say that a sentence of a spoken language is empirically meaningful if and only if it is translatable into an empirically pure language. This proposal invites a good deal of scepticism about the pure language, but quite aside from that, we run into a new bogey which in subsequent chapters will assume horrific proportions. As Hempel expresses it in some remarks made later, 'The notion of translatability needed in this context is by no means fully clear, and an attempt to explicate it faces considerable difficulties' (*LP*, p. 128). This, we shall find, was the understatement of the decade.

The unstatability of something as influential as the verification principle may be only a curiosity. We have been superfi-

---

7. Review of the second edition of *Language, Truth and Logic*, *Journal of Symbolic Logic*, XIV (1949), 52-3.
8. 'The Empiricist Criterion of Meaning' (1950: augmented 1959), *LP*, pp. 108-29.

cial, ignoring the thought underlying the principle. Schlick's papers provide the best way to understand the motivation for the principle. They recall that Wittgenstein at the time was insistent that meaning is to be given in terms of truth conditions, and more generally, as Schlick puts it in 'Meaning and Verification', 'Stating the meaning of a sentence amounts to stating the rules according to which the sentence is to be used, and this is the same as stating the way in which it can be verified (or falsified).' The final clause seems lame, indeed to be mistaken. Telling how to use the sentence 'This marigold is orange' is not the same as telling how to verify it. Yet this intermingling of ideas lent a good deal of survival-value to our doomed verification principle. And much survived the overt principle. For example, Schlick had a truly remarkable answer to our question Why does language matter to philosophy?

The great contemporary turning point is characterized by the fact that we see in philosophy not a system of cognitions, but a system of *acts*; Philosophy is that activity through which the meaning of statements is revealed or determined . . . Bestowing meaning upon statements cannot be done in turn by statements . . . the final giving of meaning always takes place, therefore, through *deeds*. It is these deeds or acts that constitute philosophical activity.[9]

9. 'The Turning Point in Philosophy' (1930), *LP*, pp. 56-7.

10. Norman Malcolm's dreams

The first generation of verificationists sought to eliminate metaphysics wholesale by a single application of a single criterion. The second generation recognized that the verificationist attitude could not be summed up in a single formula. The verification principle collapsed as soon as it was stated. Yet the attitude might still be applied to individual problems. Each problem, it could be agreed, had its own pathology, but most would yield to a deft and individual verificationist treatment. Some of the problems were new, engendered by a new science or technology, but others were old. Few problems of epistemology are more ancient than the sceptical doubt we examine in this chapter, 'Is it possible that with all the experiences before me as I seem to write these words, I am in fact dreaming?' Plato presents it with his customary elegance:

Socrates. I think that you must often have heard persons ask: – How can you determine whether at this moment we are sleeping, and all our thoughts are a dream; or whether we are awake, and talking to one another in the waking state?

Theaetetus. Indeed, Socrates, I do not know how to prove the one any more than the other, for in both cases the facts precisely correspond; and there is no difficulty in supposing that during all this discussion we have been talking to one another in a dream; and when in a dream we seem to be narrating dreams, the resemblance of the two states is quite astonishing.

Socrates. You see, then, that a doubt about the reality of sense is easily raised, since there may even be a doubt whether we are awake or in a dream. (*Theaetetus*, 158)

Socrates' question has diverted epistemologists ever since. The Cartesian *ego*, trapped in its world of ideas, was especially vulnerable. Some of its narrative sequences of ideas correspond to no reality; they are dreams. How can I tell that all such narratives are not dreams? How do I know I am not dreaming right now, as I write these words?

One common answer is that the experiences of waking life have a coherence that dreams lack. It is not logically impossible that our dreams should be as coherent, but as a matter of fact they hang together only briefly and locally. For all practical purposes we can nearly always tell at once which experiences are merely dreamt. Leibniz, for example, thought that one could not reasonably ask for more and found Socrates' question boring. From time to time, however, some philosophers have attempted a more definitive answer. Descartes is the most celebrated. The most recent is Norman Malcolm.[1]

According to Malcolm we should not seek to answer the question 'Am I dreaming now?' with an infallible negation, but rather show that the question itself does not make sense. The sceptic is not to be answered, but to have the very rug of his question drawn out from under his feet. The argument is verificationist. A question makes sense only if the words expressing both affirmative and negative answers to it make sense. Malcolm contends that 'I am dreaming now' does not make sense. The root idea of the argument is this: a sentence makes sense if and only if it is possible to verify that somebody understands the meaning of it. We must determine, for example, whether he will assert it, under suitable questioning, when it is true, and deny it when it is false. Now the fact that a man asserting something is itself evidence that he is awake. Hence assertion of 'I am dreaming now' is self-refuting. So there are no conditions under which one can truly assert the

---

1. In the present chapter page references are to Norman Malcolm, *Dreaming* (London: Routledge and Kegan Paul; New York: Humanities Press, 1959).

sentence. *A fortiori*, we can never verify that a man asserts it when it is true. Hence the sentence does not make sense.

This argument is a little bald. Even if our sceptic cannot truly *assert* that he is dreaming, because asserting implies being awake, he might truly think he is dreaming, and afterwards tell us so. If we could check that he were dreaming at the specified time, we should have verified his correct use of the sentence, and thus, perhaps, the first person present tense sentence 'I am dreaming' might be allowed some sense, at least in the thought of the dreamer. To counter this plausible move, Malcolm uses the verb 'to judge' as a portmanteau covering thinking, opining, believing, concluding, inferring, and the like. He must show that I cannot judge (think, infer, etc.) that I am dreaming. The argument has two branches. First, I cannot judge that I am asleep; second, I cannot make any judgment while I am asleep.

Judgment seems to take us from the spoken word to mental discourse. A philosopher of an earlier era took it for granted that mental discourse can be significant in its own right. Far from being parasitic on public speech, it is prior to what is public. The new grip of verificationism has turned this upside down. Statements about mental events can be verified only by observing non-mental events and abilities and tendencies, including public speech acts. The mental life becomes parasitic on the world of public affairs. Malcolm says,

I will raise the question of whether it can be verified that someone *understands* how to use the sentence 'I am asleep' to describe his own state. If there is that use of the sentence it ought to make sense to verify that someone has or has not mastered it. (p. 9)

A direct verification would be determining that the person commonly asserts 'I am asleep' when he is asleep, but if we took him to be making an assertion we should thereby take him to be awake. So that method of verification is not open. An alternative is 'projecting' the meaning from the meanings of other sentences. For example, we all know what 'He is asleep' means. We can readily display our ability to use that sentence correctly, and thereby convince Malcolm that we understand it. Moreover for many properties *P* there appears to be a standard connection between the meaning of 'He is *P*' and 'I am *P*', namely, that the latter ascribes to me the same property that the former ascribed to him. Hence, if I understand a sentence of one form, surely I understand the other as well? Malcolm rejects this argument, reasoning as follows. We tell that someone else is asleep by observing a relaxed body, regular breathing (or perhaps nightmare tension and tossing); he tends not to notice moderate sounds and events around him. But I can hardly apply these criteria to myself to find out if I am asleep! Since the criteria for 'He is asleep' do not transform by merely grammatical changes on the pronoun into criteria for my being asleep, we cannot infer understanding of 'I am asleep' from understanding of 'He is asleep.' This argument is a somewhat deeper form of verificationism than any noted in the previous chapter. There we had Schlick: 'Stating the meaning of a sentence amounts to stating the rules according to which the sentence is to be used, and this is the same as stating the way in which it can be verified.' To get the rules for use, 'we want a description of the conditions under which the sentence will form a *true* proposition and of those which will make it *false*'. Malcolm adds a further clause: the way in which the sentence is to be verified depends not just on the truth conditions, but on our criteria for telling when the truth conditions are satisfied. Criteria for telling when 'He is asleep' is true cannot move on to criteria for telling when 'I am asleep' is true. Hence we cannot project the meaning from 'He is asleep' on to 'I am asleep.'

Another candidate for projection, 'I was asleep', succumbs to the same argument; the criteria for saying that I was asleep could hardly be applied in sleep:.

Nor could I reason as follows: 'They tell me that I was asleep just now; so by remembering what my state was, I shall be able to identify future states of myself as states of sleep.' For what is it exactly that I am supposed to remember? Not some condition of my body: I cannot be supposed to identify in that way a present state of mine as sleep. Not some conscious experience, for the reason already given. The memory of my state of sleep turns out to be an unintelligible notion, since nothing can be plausibly suggested as the *content* of the memory. (pp. 12–13)

Abandoning both direct verification and projection, Malcolm finds himself forced to conclude that 'Neither I nor anyone else can find out whether the state of myself that I claim to describe by the sentence "I am asleep", really is the state of being asleep. The possibility of finding this out must be rejected as a conceptual absurdity. . . Which is to say that a judgment that one is asleep is not an intelligible notion' (pp. 13–14). Had a student of Kant's *Critique of Pure Reason* sought to show that I cannot judge I am asleep, he would have argued that some concepts are impossible; critical philosophy in the verificationist style says the judgment is impossible because there can be no words to express it. We see the switch from concepts to words even more readily in the second branch of Malcolm's discussion:

Arguing fom the impossibility of judging that one is asleep we arrive at an important result, namely, that it is nonsensical to suppose that while a person is asleep he could make *any* judgment . . . In order to know that he had made any judgment [while asleep] one would have to know that he had said certain words and that he had been aware of saying them. But whatever it was in his demeanour that revealed his awareness of saying them would also establish that he was not asleep . . . It would be self-contradictory to verify that he made *any* judgment while asleep . . . If a sleeping person could note that it is raining or judge that his wife is jealous, then why could he not judge that he is asleep? The absurdity of the latter proves the absurdity of the former. (pp. 35–6)

Malcolm acknowledges that this 'proof' is weak, because at best it shows 'that the *verification* that someone is both asleep and judging is self-contradictory, not that his *being* both asleep and judging is self-contradictory'. Malcolm contends that being both asleep and judging is however "senseless in the sense that nothing can count in favour of either its truth or its falsity' (p. 37).

But this conclusion simply does not follow from the impossibility of judging that one is asleep. Malcolm must prove that nothing can count in favour of the claim that I judged when asleep. There can be no direct evidence: I cannot judge 'I am asleep and am now judging that $23 \times 6 = 138$', for I cannot judge that I am asleep. But perhaps a man can infer from other data that he judged while sleeping. One possibility is that he made the judgment at the same time he heard some external event – a clap of thunder – an event occurring at the specific time when he was asleep. No, says Malcolm, since this implies that he heard thunder, 'the conclusion to be drawn is that he was not fully asleep when it thundered and not that he made a judgment while fully asleep' (p. 38). Malcolm made clear earlier that his topic was really 'sound sleep' only. Incidentally, this somewhat diminishes Malcolm's attack on Descartes, for Descartes was fully aware that 'whenever we have a dream that we afterwards remember, that means we are sleeping only lightly'[2] Presumably Descartes raises the problem of dreaming for epistemology specifically for 'light sleep' whereas Malcolm has wilfully restricted himself to 'sound sleep'!

Disregarding the question about sound sleep, we are driven to one critical issue. Clearly the best candidate for judging when asleep is judging in dreams. Malcolm does not contend that I cannot correctly say, 'In my dream I judged that my wife is jealous.' For he holds that the practice of what he calls telling a dream gives sense to any expression 'In my dream it happened that p', where p itself makes sense only in waking life. His thought is more radical. He holds that there is no particular time at which one can say that one dreamt. *A for-*

2. In a letter to Antoine Arnauld dated 29 July 1648, trans. in *Descartes, Philosophical Letters,* ed. and trans. Anthony Kenny (Oxford: University Press, 1970), p. 233.

tiori there is no time at which one judged so one did not judge when asleep. The situation is that on waking one tells dreams, and thinks that the dream happened in sleep. But, Malcolm contends, there is no way of verifying at what particular time the dream occurred. 'Are we to understand "at the same time" in objective physical time? As measured for example by the clock or the rising of the moon? If so, what possible grounds could one have for such an assertion?' Malcolm wants us to have no grounds, but two naturally occur.

First, there is the experience, familiar to many tellers of dreams, of incorporating into the dream elements of the world – noises or a drop in temperature. But this won't do. For suppose in a dream I have transformed the sound of bicycle bells ringing outside a busy window into Swiss cowbells. I claim these bells date my Alpine dream as coincident with the early morning fracas with bicycles. But how do I know that I did not e.g. simply 'remember' the bells and build this into my dream half an hour later? As there is no way of telling whether my first hypothesis or this rival hypothesis of memory is correct, neither (in Malcolm's radical epistemology) can be an hypothesis about any matter of fact at all.

There are, however, data of quite a different kind, of which there are now a good many popular résumés. Sleep, it has been discovered, is cyclic. There are periods of deep sleep when the body is extremely passive, and periods of activity which show up most notably in 'rapid eye movement', which is not dissimilar to the eye movement of an alert spectator at a football match. Moreover periods of rapid eye movement are strongly correlated with the subsequent telling of dreams. For instance, if a subject is always woken just as he is coming out of the passive period into the active one, he tells no dreams; if he is woken in the middle of a period of REM, he says: I was just dreaming about levitating, detecting spies, burying my mother, or whatever. Research workers consider that by now they have amply corroborated the hypothesis that dreams can be accurately dated by observed REM. Indeed, there is considerable correlation between the kind of eye movement and the content of the dream; the eyes move in the way they would if they were actually watching scenes reported by the dreamer.

Malcolm scrupulously considers this evidence and accepts that we may come to adopt REM as a criterion for dating dreams. But, says Malcolm, this is not a case of adopting a 'decision' to use the words 'I dreamt at 11.30 but not at 1.45' in a certain way. 'It would certainly be overwhelmingly natural for us to adopt this *convention*', says Malcolm (p. 76), but it is still a convention that we are free to adopt or reject. Far from confirming an hypothesis the students of dreams 'are proposing a new concept in which the notions of location and duration of dreams in physical time and the subjective–objective distinction will have a place' (p. 81). 'A new concept would have been created that only remotely resembled the old one.'

Most readers, unreflectively, are very surprised at Malcolm's conclusion, and a good many continue to be surprised even after serious reflection. The issue, which seems so specific to dreaming, is in fact very general, and in other contexts will come to dominate the next chapter, which concerns currently fundamental issues in the philosophy of science. For example in his critique of Malcolm, Hilary Putnam invites us to ask the same question about the word 'acid' that Malcolm asks about 'dream'.[3] Chemists spoke of acids in 1800 and they do so now. Acids were detected by the way in which they entered into a fairly small range of reactions, of which the most familiar is the litmus paper test. Subsequently, titration using phenolphthalein provided a more sensitive test and an actual measure of degree of acidity. More important, we have come to understand much better what acids are; they

---

3. 'Dreaming and Depth Grammar', *Analytical Philosophy*, Series 1, ed. R. Butler (Oxford: Blackwell, 1962), pp. 211-35.

are compounds containing an atom that can accept a pair of electrons from a base. This explains the phenomenal classification of 1800, in which an acid was something that could neutralize a base. Common sense would say we have found out more and more about acids. John Dalton (1766–1844), often called the founder of the atomic theory of chemistry, knew very little of what we know, but among other things he, like a modern chemist, was concerned with acids. Most of the things we now call acids he would have called acids, but not altogether. We have better means of detection, but we also have new theoretical reasons for calling things acids. It is true that he would have defined 'acid' differently from any high school student today, but he himself saw his work partly as discovering the essence of acidity, that is, of working towards a correct definition of a phenomenally recognizable natural kind. He meant by 'acid' what we do, even though he would have defined it less well.

Someone who agrees with Malcolm can hardly accept this account. We have new criteria for recognizing acids; moreover the criteria are often different in kind, for they are of a far more theoretical nature. Ought we to speak of conventions and decisions? Ought we to insist that what you and I mean by 'acid' is something different from what John Dalton meant? This turns out to be a substantial question, transcending Malcolm's dreams.

Putnam has, of course, a number of specific criticisms of Malcolm's theory of meaning, and is especially critical of his sentence-by-sentence way of attaching meaning to sentences. He rejects Malcolm's refusal to project meaning for 'I am dreaming' on the basis of other similar grammatical structures, and other sentences using the verb 'to dream'. In this he is much influenced by the work of Chomsky to which we have alluded in Chapters 6 and 8. An algorithm that will show that the sentence 'I am dreaming' is grammatical should enable one to project the meaning for that sentence. Malcolm must show, indeed, that 'I am dreaming' is ungrammatical, which is a tall order. But these specific objections may be left aside. For the dispute between Putnam and Malcolm, about 'dreaming at time *t*' or 'acid', leads us on to matters vastly more serious than dreaming or acids. Indeed, in the past four chapters we have been describing a few cases of work done in what we may call 'the heyday of meanings'. Towards the end of the preceding chapter we quoted Hempel saying that a notion of translatability is not entirely clear, and faces considerable difficulties. Now we find a problem about whether theoretical advance changes meaning by producing new criteria, or simply lets us find out more about dreams and acids. These innocent questions presage the end of the heyday of meanings. That is the subject of the next part of the book.

C. The heyday of sentences

11. Paul Feyerabend's theories

Theories about what kinds of things there are in the universe occur in almost all our case studies. Berkeley was sure that matter does not exist. The verificationists gladly accepted the view that 'ontology recapitulates epistemology' – in particular, what you can't know about, isn't. Now we must touch on another question about existence, not so much 'What kinds of things are there in the universe?' as 'To what extent are the kinds of objects that exist dependent upon the theories and presuppositions of the society for whom they exist?' I deliberately put the question in a paradoxical way. The immediate answer to this last question is: the existence of objects is in no way dependent upon the theories that we hold! There is, however, a good question lurking beneath the bad one, but because I do not know quite how to ask it I follow the traditional philosophical technique of overasking.

We ended the last chapter with a debate between Malcolm and Putnam, as to whether 'acid' in the eighteenth century means the same as 'acid' nowadays, or 'dream' means the same before and after REM. We approach dangerously near to the stupid question (which, alas, is actually raised in some quarters) of whether acids in the eighteenth century are the same as they are now. As far as the word 'acid' is concerned, we had Putnam, on the one hand, robustly proclaiming that we have found out more about acids, but that we are still talking about the same kind of thing, and using words in the same ways, as our predecessors. On the other hand, a generalization of Malcolm's argument about dreams suggests the opposite doctrine, that since we have discovered new criteria for acidity, so we mean something different from John Dalton. So far this is a potentially boring controversy but if we extend the scope of discussion we get surprising results. Remember that the chief difference in chemistry in 1800 and now is not that we have new methods of testing for and measuring acidity, but that we have chemical theories of which even the 'founder of the atomic theory of chemistry' perceived at most a very feeble glimmer. 'Acid' is now so embedded in theory that there is more ground for saying that the word no longer means the same. We must embark on a theory of theories. Let us proceed systematically, first setting out a *thesis* and then an *antithesis*. The thesis represents what has, in much of this century, been received philosophy of science. The antithesis will be a new and somewhat revolutionary attack on the thesis.

In theorizing we need the benefit of language not only to communicate with others but also to record our own thoughts. Language is essential to human theorizing, but (says the thesis) it is the tool of the theory. In digging my garden I occasionally break a spade and buy a new one. More gradually the edge of my spade becomes worn and ragged while the wooden shaft becomes smooth. Digging does affect spades, but a spade is a spade for all that, an entity in its own right, whether I dig or let it rust. Such a relationship (it is urged) is the one holding between language and theory. We use our languages to speculate, but they exist in their own right, somewhat low on the chain of being, at the level of spades. They are not much affected by theorizing, but they are, like spades, somewhat affected, and occasionally, there is a snapping shaft, a scientific revolution, and we opt for a whole new language.

According to the thesis scientific enquiry has a fairly simple logical structure. What goes on in laboratory, classroom, journal, and over coffee may be erratic, but the finished product can be recast into a tidy deductive structure. Thus theories must explain what has been observed to happen. Explanation is deductive, for we explain by showing that what happened is a logical consequence of our theories plus some specific antecedent conditions. Theories also predict what will happen. Prediction is equally deductive; we deduce from the theory that if experiment E is made a definite (perhaps surprising) result R follows. Success in explanation and variety in prediction are two of the virtues of the best theories. Deduction is the keynote of both.

The thesis readily accounts for incompatible theories in the same domain. There are two sets of speculations, one of which implies that if experiment E is made, then result R will occur, while the other speculations imply that R will not come out of E. The way to decide between the two theories is to perform E and see whether R occurs or not. This is the 'crucial experiment', which has long been part of the theory of theories.

Crucial experiments constitute one kind of scientific progress. Another kind of theoretical advance is the subsumption of one theory under a more general one. For example, Snell's law states a relation between the angle of incidence and the angle of refraction when a light-ray is bent on passing from one medium (such as air) to another (such as water). Fermat (1601–65) showed that Snell's law is a consequence of the proposition that light follows the quickest route. This was duly subsumed under more general laws of physical optics, which can in turn be derived as consequences of quantum mechanics. This, according to the thesis, is a clear-cut case of subsumption. Quantum mechanics employs theoretical machinery undreamt of by Snell or Fermat, but Snell's law, as derived in quantum mechanics, is the very same law that Snell hit upon empirically.

Let us repeat that according to the thesis, language although essential for theorizing plays no profound part in the theory of theories. Naturally, we must be able to report the outcome of a crucial experiment in words. There must be a sentence, scholarly paper, or even a book *r* which says that experiment *E* was performed at a specific time and place, and result *R* occurred, and there must be a contrary possible report *r**, saying *E* was made at the stated time and place but *R* did not occur. If we believe *r*, we conclude that the second theory is wrong, while if we believe *r** we believe that the first theory is wrong. Were it not for sentences like *r* and *r** there would be no science transmitted from generation to generation nor from laboratory to laboratory. Equally we could not talk of subsuming Snell's law under quantum mechanics were there not a sentence expressing what Snell meant in 1621 and which also expresses a consequence of the quantum theory. Language is indispensable, yes, but we hardly need a theory of language to understand science.

Yet the thesis does invite one query about language. Sophisticated theories appear to speak of theoretical entities, such as electrons or genes, which, at the time of promulgating the theory, cannot possibly be observed. The entities are postulated in order to explain phenomena. Even if we take the meaning of terms in common speech for granted, we may demand an account of the meaning of the theoretical terminology that has evolved in such profusion in the past few centuries. We cannot indicate the meaning of the word 'electron' by pointing. Nor can we glibly say that its meaning is given by its 'use' in the theory, because we may have different theories about electrons; what in one theory is a use of the word 'electron' to state a fundamental postulate may, in another theory, be a use to express a contrast with something now outmoded. Writing in the 1920s Norman Campbell solved (or shelved) this problem about meaning by injecting another element into the rational reconstruction of completed theories. On the one hand we have a set of hypotheses, the fundamental tenets of the theory. These will typically involve theoretical terms. No experiment will enable us to observe directly whether these are true, because the objects in question, theoretical entities, are not observable at all. Hence we require some way to hook up the deeper parts of the theory with surface observation. Campbell suggested a 'dictionary' to fill in the deductive links between any theory using a set of theoretical terms and a body of possible observation reports. The dictionary tells us what to expect if the theory is true. Language then becomes dichotomized: there are potential reports of observations, and there are theoretical statements; the two parts are linked by the 'dictionary' that enables us to deduce observations from axioms.

A theory is a connected set of propositions which are divided into two groups. One group consists of statements about some collection of ideas which are characteristic of the theory; the other group consists of statements of the relation between these ideas and some other ideas of a different nature. The first group will be termed collectively the 'hypothesis' of the theory; the second group the 'dictionary'. The hypothesis is so called, in accordance with the sense that has just been stated, because the propositions composing it are incapable of proof or of disproof by themselves; they must be significant, but, taken apart from the dictionary, they appear arbitrary assumptions. They may be considered accordingly as providing a 'definition by postulate' of the ideas which are characteristic of the hypothesis. The ideas which are related by means of the dictionary to the ideas of the hypothesis are, on the other hand, such that something is known about them apart from the theory. It must be possible to determine, apart from all knowledge of the theory, whether certain propositions involving these ideas are true or false.[1]

Campbell, himself a minor experimental physicist, is only one of many who discuss the methodology of science in these terms, at about this time. Note that already in his work the crucial experiment is no longer simple in structure. We have two incompatible theories, T_1 and T_2, using between them a body of theoretical terms. The theories do not in themselves

---

1. *Physics: the Elements* (Cambridge: University Press, 1920); reprinted as *Foundations of Science: The Philosophy of Theory and Experiment* (New York: Dover, 1957), p. 122.

entail the contrary observation reports r and $r*$; they do so only with the aid of a Campbellian 'dictionary'. It is not claimed that actual scientific textbooks look like this; only that this is the way we would rewrite them if we wanted to be thoroughly rigorous.

The thesis, in its strongest forms, was for long entrenched in the Vienna Circle, and one of its most stringent expositors was Rudolf Carnap. Like his contemporaries he was convinced of a sharp distinction between theoretical and observation terms. The two are related by some kind of Campbellian dictionary. The meanings of theoretical terms are fairly constant; when there is a change, it will be represented by a change in the dictionary. There is a sharp contrast between changing theories and changing meanings. Scientific growth is typically of two sorts: (a) refutation of a theory and its replacement by another, often as a result of a crucial experiment, and (b) subsumption of one theory under a more general one.

The antithesis to this thesis denies all these doctrines. Let us begin at the sharp distinction between observation and theory. A word coined by N. R. Hanson is useful here: he urges that our descriptive, observational terms are 'theory-laden'. That is, we apply them specifically in the light of the theories and laws that we happen to subscribe to. Certainly knowledge of theory is essential to an example Hanson uses: 'an X-ray tube viewed from the cathode'.[2] Unskilled help in the lab can sort X-ray tubes from rheostats, but must be taught ultimately by someone knowing a little theory, and moreover, sorting is only one thing concepts are for. To determine whether a dubious object really is a new-model X-ray tube or not, one has to know what it does, and that cannot be explained except in theoretical terms.

There are two distinct points here. One is that what we say we see at any moment is itself often determined by our

2. *Patterns of Discovery* (Cambridge: University Press, 1965), p. 15.

knowledge. Even Plato could urge this in the *Theaetetus*, where a scholar and an illiterate are shown some writing. They have good eyesight and one is tempted to say that they see the same thing. Yet at the very least the scholar sees more: he sees the word 'rose'. No matter how poor a calligrapher he is he can re-present what he has seen so that we see the word 'rose'. But illiterates typically cannot even recognize the word when presented again. Likewise the motor mechanic hears that the timing is wrong, when I hear only a noise from the engine. The pilot feels a vertical updraught when I feel only a lurch. The archeologist sees neolithic pottery where I see only scattered shards. Or, to take a striking example claimed by Hanson, a good undergraduate student of physics can see the track of the positron in a cloud chamber placed in a magnetic field, and yet the chief physicists of the 1920s could not see such a thing even when 'it was before their very eyes' and duly recorded on photographs.[3]

Such examples call in question naive beliefs about 'direct perception'. A second point is that direct perception, even if there is such a thing, has only a little to do with the application of words. No matter how sure I am that I see a brick in the path, if it explodes when I pick it up, then I never saw a brick, no matter how much I 'directly perceived'. Part of our theory of bricks is that although they can be used as offensive missiles, real bricks do not explode like bombs. Our use of a descriptive term, be it 'brick' or 'cathode', depends on our taking for granted some supposed constancies in nature. Only very general statements of constancies are dignified with the name 'theory', but our antithesis holds that although there are degrees of the load of theory borne by a descriptive term, we have no difference in kind, in this respect, between cathode-ray tubes and bricks.

Discussions as to whether there is pure 'seeing' unladen by theory tend to become nebulous. Upholders of the thesis con-

3. *The Concept of the Positron* (Cambridge: University Press, 1963).

tend that the pilot and I alike feel the lurch; he 'infers' there is a vertical updraught. The archeologist and I alike see how the shards look; he infers from this look that they are neolithic. The best physicist in the 1920s and an undergraduate of today see similar tracks; our modern student has been trained to infer the positron. Such a debate becomes substantial only when we take in other elements of the thesis among which the reconstruction into 'hypothesis' and 'dictionary' is an obvious weak point. Scientific work is never in fact so dichotomized, and it is seldom clear that there is a unique way of splitting up the theory into hypothesis and dictionary. In particular, a revision in a theory can be presented either as a change in the dictionary, which preserves the laws, or a change in the laws, using the same dictionary. Which is the 'right' reconstruction? Such a query leads back to our illustrative starting point: have we found out more about acids, still meaning the same by 'acid', or has the growth of knowledge led to a change in the very meaning of the word 'acid'?

To maintain its position, the thesis, at first so indifferent to 'meaning', now requires some criterion for change in meaning of theoretical terms. The best evidence that a term has changed in meaning is, perhaps, that it is used differently. In theoretical speculation we are chiefly concerned with declarative utterances (and the corresponding questions) usually offered as attempts to say what is true. So it is especially natural to follow Frege, and say that the truth conditions for a sentence determine the meaning of a sentence, and that the meaning of a term is settled by the meaning of the sentences in which it can occur. Let us pretend, with the thesis, that there is a definite set of observation sentences whose truth conditions are well understood, independent of theory. Then, given a dictionary, we can also determine truth conditions of theoretical hypotheses. For the thesis, the dichotomy into theoretical and observation sentences, and the dichotomy into dictionary and hypotheses, are both crucial. If both divisions are artificial, the thesis is endangered, because truth conditions for sentences involving theoretical terms are themselves dependent on the theoretical contexts in which they occur. 'The distribution of electrons is 50 per cent spin-up, 50 per cent spin-down' has no standard use outside some version of the quantum theory. It has no truth conditions apart from the theory, and hence, on a simplistic version of the Fregean account, no meaning either. Indeed, one need not reason from any particular theory of meaning to this conclusion; here for example is Norman Campbell again:

many of the words used in expressing scientific laws denote ideas which depend for their significance on the truth of certain other laws and would lose all meaning if those laws were not true. These words include most of the technical terms of science . . . they will in future be called 'concepts'. *A concept is a word denoting an idea which depends for its meaning or significance on the truth of some law.* The conclusion at which we have arrived is that most, if not all, of the recognised laws of physics state relations between concepts, and not between simple judgements of sensation which remain significant even if no relation between them is known. (*Foundations of Science*, p. 45; my italics)

The passage that I have italicized, written fifty years ago, has consequences that have only been developed in the past decade. If the meaning of the theoretical terms or 'concepts' depends on the laws and theories, what happens when we revise or abandon the law or a theory? The radical conclusion drawn by the antithesis is that meanings change. Moreover if the same term occurs in two different theories, we seem driven to the conclusion that the term differs in meaning in the two contexts. This has disastrous consequences for the central tenets of the thesis. Theoretical progress cannot occur by deductive subsumption of one theory under another, for that requires sentences meaning the same in both stronger and weaker theories, and that now seems ruled out. Even the crucial experiment founders. Here is a vivid statement of that possibility, by Paul Feyerabend:

a crucial experiment is now impossible. It is impossible not because the experimental device would be too complex or expensive, but because there is no universally accepted statement capable of expressing whatever emerges from observation.[4]

The antithesis in short holds that rival or successive theories in the same domain are incomparable or incommensurable. The actual word 'incommensurable', which has attained something of a vogue in the past few years, was introduced in the 1960s, by Feyerabend and by Thomas Kuhn. Kuhn, the distinguished historian of science, has urged in his now famous book *The Structure of Scientific Revolutions* that there are sharp discontinuities between successive or competing scientific theories, of a sort for which there are few 'rational' ways of choosing between them. I do not here wish to develop this much-contested branch of the philosophy of science, but to notice only the alleged consequences for theories of meaning. In the case of the crucial experiment, Feyerabend, in the passage quoted, asserts that there exists no theoretical sentence with a definite meaning which is true in one theory and in the very same sense is false in the other. There is no way of translating between theories.

Such a conclusion seems monstrous. One can think of a few incommensurable theories 'in the same domain'. Freudian psychoanalysis and the stimulus–response theory in behavioural psychology study the human psyche, but quite literally Freudians and s–r psychologists do not talk to each other; in a sense they cannot. Likewise contemporary Chinese acupuncture enables Chinese surgeons to perform a wide range of operations on fully conscious patients who are actually able to guide the scalpel of the surgeon and yet feel little discomfort. Western surgeons use total anaesthetics for the same operations. At present, acupuncture theory makes hardly any sense at all in Western medical theory. A few of its phenomena are beginning to be 'explained' but its concepts cannot

4. 'Problems of Empiricism', in *Beyond the Edge of Certainty*, ed. R. Colodny (Englewood Cliffs, N.J.: Prentice–Hall, 1965), p. 214.

even be expressed. For another example, it has long been urged by anthropologists that one cannot comprehend theories of witchcraft without learning the language and perhaps even adopting the way of life of the Zande people (or whoever).

Yet the thesis is hardly moved by bizarre examples like these. It need not claim that all theories in 'the same domain' are commensurable; only that much orderly scientific progress concerns the rivalry or accumulation of commensurable theories. All our folklore assures us that the thesis is right about this. As it happens, however, folklore is not a perfect guide. Recent research in the history of science displays more incommensurability than had been expected. One of the classic examples of 'subsumption' used to be classical Newtonian mechanics in the relativistic mechancis of Einstein. The former, we were often told, is a limiting case of the latter, and we have a good example of subsumption. Feyerabend has argued persuasively that the concepts of Newtonian mechanics are simply inexpressible in relativity theory. At the same time it must be clear that not every adumbration of theory leads to incommensurability.

Our thesis and antithesis constitute an antinomy. Feyerabend has done as much as anyone to bring the antinomy to our notice, but has himself been little interested in it of late. He came to these problems through a dissatisfaction with the Copenhagen school of quantum mechanics. That school insisted that although new theory was needed to describe microscopic events, it should coincide with classical physics when it got round to describing macroscopic events as limiting cases. Feyerabend thought that this 'correspondence principle' is an absurd methodological limitation on research – why should the new theory say the same as the old when speaking of the same domain? Ought it not to say something new, perhaps even incompatible with the old, or, better, incommensurable with the old because arising from deeper insights? He then realized that the Copenhagen school had been constrained by a general methodology of science of which our thesis is a refined form. Then arose the generalized doctrine of incommensurability we have just described. But Feyerabend's interests in commensurability are not his main ones. He is in general opposed to the idea of science as systematic. Indeed his paper 'Against Method, A Defence of Anarchy' urges that the proliferation of incommensurable theories is a good thing.[5] No man can think himself into more than one theory at the same time; let us have different workers working in the same field but unable to speak to each other. There need be no irrationality here, for different research programmes can be judged by the way in which they expand, opening new horizons, or degenerate into merely solving old puzzles that arise within their own problem area.[6] Feyerabend, creator of our antinomy, has walked away from it, proclaiming it of little interest compared with the greater problems of philosophy of science. But he has left one hint of a synthesis which will not evade our antinomy but resolve it. Both sides of our antinomy invoke a concept of meaning. But all talk about meaning, says Feyerabend of late, is mere gossip. If he is right, our antinomy hardly arises.

An antinomy is to be resolved not by siding with thesis or antithesis, but by understanding the basic error that makes the contradiction possible. According to the thesis, it must be possible to state some testable proposition which is true in one theory and false in the other. That is, there must be a sentence whose meaning is neutral between the two theories, and which, in this meaning, is true in one and false in the

5. In *Minnesota Studies in the Philosophy of Science*, iv, ed. M. Radner and S. Winokur (Minneapolis: University of Minnesota Press, 1970).
6. This approach was being developed with great panache by Imre Lakatos, who has just died in the midst of much unfinished work. In an obituary note for the Philosophy of Science Association (1974) Feyerabend has described Lakatos as the most profound student of scientific methodology in this half-century. See the bibliography for Chapter 11.

other. The antithesis protests that, according to the best theories of meaning that we have, there can be no such sentence. Feyerabend has never gone to the point of saying that any difference in theory produces a difference in meaning. For example, merely changing the numerical value of fundamental constants need not do so. But he urges that important novelties, which have to do with new lines of research characteristically produce incommensurable concepts. Many, perhaps most, philosophers have recently reacted to this by trying to produce better theories of meaning. Feyerabend is more radical, and suggests that the antinomy arises not because of an inadequate theory of meaning, but because of any theory of meaning. The basic error is to have a theory of meaning at all. We should abandon meanings and contemplate only sentences. Consider what we say, not what we mean. Consider not *statements*, i.e. sentences invested with meaning, and whose meaning may be put in question, but *sentences*. Immediately after his claim that crucial experiments are sometimes impossible, Feyerabend continues:

there is still human experience as an actually existing process, and it still causes the observer to carry out certain actions, for example, to utter sentences of a certain kind . . . This is the only way in which experience judges a general cosmological point of view. Such a point of view is not removed because its observation statements say that there must be certain experiences that then do not occur . . . It is removed if it produces observation sentences when observers produce the negation of these sentences.

What is being said here? It seems to be advice to scrap 'meanings' and forget about observation statements, i.e. sentences with meanings. There is nothing over and above certain kinds of behaviour, the uttering of sentences. Sentences certainly have syntactic structure, occasions of utterance, sites on which they appear, institutions that sanction them, theories to which they are germane, and people who are deemed fit to utter just these sentences (about the meson, say) and not those (about DNA). But – so goes the Feyerabend doctrine –

there is not something over and above these things, namely the meaning of the sentence. The observer and his experiment do not interact by way of meanings. There are only the sentences that come out of the observer's mouth or typewriter or punchcard.

The obscurity of this doctrine has not gone unnoticed[7] but this new approach to knowledge has won admirers as well as critics. Notably similar points of view have emerged from other problems. In Part B of this book, which I have called 'The Heyday of Meanings', there was always some theory of meaning in the offing. It was regularly assumed that there was something below the level of what is said: there is, in addition, what is meant. Feyerabend is one representative of a new and brazen positivism. There is nothing to language over and above what is said. Here comes the death of meaning. As is often the case when assassins have a common object, they have different motives and different styles. If Feyerabend is the Cassius of the present plot, then Davidson of the next chapter is its Brutus.

7. Dudley Shapere, 'Meaning and Scientific Change', in *Mind and Cosmos*, ed. R. Colodny (Pittsburgh, Pa.: University of Pittsburgh Press, 1966), pp. 41-85.

12. Donald Davidson's truth

Donald Davidson's work is even more inaccessible to the general reader than that of Feyerabend. He too has promised a book but at the time of writing we have only a sequence of papers scattered in journals, anthologies, and conference proceedings. These essays are uncompromisingly professional. When there is a dry half-sentence of joke it is likely to be a sign that a whole train of thought has been omitted. Thus he says wryly that one of his opinions 'can be justified by a transcendental argument (which I will not give here)'.[1] Other philosophers have recently written whole books around their transcendental arguments! These papers of Davidson are compact, allusive, half the length that is usual in contemporary journals of philosophy, and vastly more intricate. They are not easy to understand, and often take for granted quite technical results in the philosophy of logic. Hence this chapter has to be longer than most previous ones, and is broken up into sections, some of which may, in themselves, introduce the reader to a few specialist issues currently aired in analytic philosophy.

As may be seen from the bibliography for Chapter 12, Davidson's papers fall roughly into two categories. In one set

1. 'In Defense of Convention T', in *Truth, Syntax and Modality*, ed. H. Leblanc (Amsterdam: North Holland, 1973), p. 82. Some of the transcendental argument alluded to here has since appeared in 'The Very Thought of a Conceptual Scheme', *Proceedings of the American Philosophical Association*, XXII (1973), 5-29.

of titles we find such key words as *action, reason, cause, event*; the topics are chiefly drawn from the philosophy of mind. The other batch of titles has *truth, meaning, sentence, semantics*: this is the philosophy of language. Occasionally a title is constructed from both pools of key words: 'The Logical Form of Action Sentences'. The intersection is more important than the occurrence of 'action' and 'sentence' within a single title. Although Davidson seldom states the connections that he perceives between mind and semantics, he believes that the relation is essential and profound. In describing his doctrines on language I can make only passing references to his analyses of human action and I thereby omit half the story.

Davidson's best-known paper on language is 'Truth and Meaning'.[2] It is a good place to begin reading him, but before doing so you have to form some idea of an earlier body of work: Tarski's theory of truth. In a century of great logicians, no worker has had more impact on the course of mathematical logic than Alfred Tarski. The theory of truth is only one aspect of one of his investigations. Tarski gave an elementary account of it in a celebrated popular paper published in 1944 and based on results achieved more than a decade before.[3] Perhaps the most important consequences of that work lie in the mathematical discipline now called model theory, but we can abstract from it just enough to get a grip on Davidson's programme.

I. Tarski's Theory

There have been theories of truth for a long time. Tarski liked to quote Aristotle, but in thinking of his predecessors we more often refer to theories called *correspondence* and

2. *Synthese,* XVII (1967), 304-23.
3. 'The Semantic Conception of Truth and the Foundations of Semantics', *Philosophy and Phenomenological Research,* IV (1944), 341-75; reprinted for example in *Semantics and the Philosophy*

coherence. A correspondence theory says that a statement is true when it corresponds to a fact, or to the way the world is, or some such. As often as correspondence theories have been promulgated, sceptics have queried whether there is any way to characterize 'facts' independent of sentences. If not the theory appears circular. Davidson goes so far as to argue that there is only one 'fact', or one entity called 'the facts', thereby reducing the theory to absurdity. He does think that there is something right about correspondence, as we shall see, but not correspondence to facts. Other philosophers more radically abandon 'facts' and substitute 'coherence' for 'correspondence'. A coherence theory is holistic. That is to say, it does not think of truths coming along one by one, each corresponding to its own private fact. Truth, it says, has to do with an entire corpus of sentences, which must be internally consistent, and which is governed chiefly by the tendency of speakers to add or withdraw statements from this corpus in the light of their experiences.

Manifestly such 'theories of truth,' at least as I describe them, lack most of the features of clarity, precision, and predictive power that a theory ought to have. They are at best vague mumblings awaiting serious definition. We can illustrate the inadequacy of the very contrast, coherence correspondence, by recalling that many scholars have stated, with intense conviction, that Spinoza held a correspondence theory of truth. Others have urged, with comparable passion, that he held a correspondence theory! Spinoza is quite a difficult philosopher but on this occasion the fault lies not in Spinoza but in those pale and vaporous categories correspondence and coherence.

Tarski brought some rigour to truth. His idea is so simple that at first sight it appears trivial. He stated a minimum criterion to be satisfied by any theory of truth. Davidson calls it 'Convention T'. It comes in two parts. Suppose we are constructing a theory of truth for a language L (German, say), and that we are stating the theory in English. Our first requirement is that for every sentence s of L there is a provable theorem of our theory of the form:

(T)　　The sentence s of L is true if and only if p.

In any particular instance, s is replaced by the name of a sentence in L, and p by an English sentence, as in

(1)　　The German sentence 'Schnee ist weiss' is true if and only if snow is white.

Our first requirement on a theory of truth is, then that it should give us a batch of axioms and rules of inference from which we can deduce, for any sentence s of L, a corresponding T-sentence like (1). Our second requirement is that every such provable T-sentence should in fact be true – as is, in fact, the case with (1). We do not even demand that L should differ substantially from English or whatever language we are speaking, for we could try to construct a so-called homophonic theory of truth for English in English, leading us to the seemingly silly T-sentence that Tarski made famous:

(2)　　The English sentence 'Snow is white' is true if and only if snow is white.

The bite, in our pair of requirements, comes with the constraint that for each sentence s of L, it be possible to prove a corresponding T-sentence. Our examples (1) and (2) are trifling but the constraint is serious. An axiomatic theory must have a finite base. That is, it must have a finite number of axioms and a finite number of rules of inference (or at any rate a finite set of instructions for mechanically generating the axioms and rules). But there is no upper bound on the number of sentences of a language. For each s in L, our theory must provide a proof of a corresponding T-sentence.

Since there are infinitely many *s*, this means that our finite base must be able to prove an infinite number of *T*-sentences.

What could such a finite basis be? To begin with there are only finitely many simple predicates, relations, and names in a language – not many more than in a good dictionary. These can be grammatically strung together to form short simple sentences. A theory of truth could therefore begin by listing a finite number of axioms for these. If on our analysis the English sentence 'Snow is white' is one of the basic sentences then (2) would appear as an axiom. We would hope for a more economical and insightful approach, with a single rubric for all mass nouns (snow, water, lead, air, etc.), another for count nouns (hand, blade, cow) and so on. But however we have got to (2) we shall require rules to derive (*T*) for complex sentences. Sometimes this is easy. When our connective 'and' is put between two sentences it gives a third sentence. A suitable *T*-rule might be,

(3)   If sentence *s* is true if and only if *p*, and sentence *r* is true if and only if *q*, then sentence *s⌢and⌢r* is true if and only if *p* and *q*.

Here '*s⌢and⌢r*' denotes the result of writing *s*, then 'and', then *r* (and of course deleting the stop after *s*, and putting the first letter of *r* in lower case unless it commences a proper name). With (2), (3), and an axiom for 'Grass is purple' we are able to prove:

(4)   The sentence 'Snow is white and grass is purple' is true if and only if snow is white and grass is purple.

Notice that from a finite stock of sentences such as (1), augmented by the rule (3), we can derive infinitely many sentences simply by applying rule (3) over and over again, generating longer and longer conjunctions, albeit repetitive (*s* & *r* & *r* & *s* . . .). We can handle a potential infinity of these. So we have already gone one tiny step towards achieving our aim of providing a finite basis for the unbounded number of sentences of a language. Tarski's ingenuity enabled him to do something far more important in the same direction. He gave rules for 'some' and 'all', akin to (3), that lead to very deep waters. They provide a theory of truth for first-order logic, the essence of all modern symbolic logic. His approach employs a concept of 'satisfaction by a sequence', that began one of the chief frontal advances of modern logical theory. Too many new techniques are needed to summarize even that much of Tarski's work here. Davidson thinks it also enables us to make sense of a correspondence theory of truth. Truth arises not from a correspondence between sentences and facts, but from the ways in which our words are hooked up with the world ('snow' with snow) and by certain conventional devices that can be explicated within the theory of truth using Tarski's concept of 'satisfaction'. The thing to emphasize now, however, is not the nature of these elaborations, but the two simple requirements of Convention T. A theory of truth for L must be such that (i) for each sentence s of L a T-sentence should be provable and (ii) each such provable T-sentence should be true. We have said nothing of the latter condition, but we shall find that Davidson's account of translation hinges on it. First there are several fairly unrelated points about the Tarski theory that need a little amplification. Anyone who wants to go straight into Davidsonian truth and meaning might skip them and proceed direct to section III below.

II. Problems and extensions

1. *Truth-in-a-language.*   Truth is truth, it will be protested, not this hybrid, 'truth-in-a-language'. Tarski ascribes truth to sentences, but are not sentences mere typographical entities? What we say on a particular occasion may be true or false; the objects of our belief may be true or false; propositions that we propound may be true or false; but (it will be asked) can sentences be properly called true or false?

As it happens Tarski wrote much of his early work in

German which has but a single word, *Satz*, that we variously translate as 'sentence', statement', or 'proposition'. *Sätze* are true, without such distinctions, so our question of what kinds of things are properly called true did not arise for Tarski. Moreover he was writing about mathematics where a sentence is used to express one and only one statement or proposition so there is no harm in using the ambiguous word *Satz*. In daily life, however, a sentence such as 'He just went out the door' may, unlike '5 + 7 = 12', on one occasion be used to say something true and an hour later to say something false; on other occasions of utterance it may not make any sense at all. So a theory of truth for a natural language, unlike one for a mathematical discourse,

must take account of the fact that many sentences vary in truth value depending on the time they are spoken, the speaker, and even, perhaps, the audience. We can accommodate this phenomenon either by declaring that it is particular utterances or speech acts, and not sentences, that have truth values, or by making truth a relation that holds between a sentence, a speaker, and a time.[4]

Some philosophers, following the lead given by J. L. Austin in his book of lectures, *How to Do Things with Words*, think that we ought first to work out a theory of speech acts, and let everything else subsequently fall into place. Davidson has the opposite strategy. First get clear about a theory of truth for sentences; then worry in more detail about when and how the sentences are said. In the end, perhaps, what is true is not the sentence but what is said by the speakers of a language. We cannot solve all problems at once. Davidson invites us to economize, direct our thoughts at that fiction 'truth-in-a-language', and subsequently we shall come to understand truth.

2. *Consistency.* Tarski was concerned with fairly formalized language of a sort suitable for mathematics and precise science. Davidson thinks that Tarski's theory is the starting

4. 'Semantics for Natural Languages', in *Linguaggi nella Società e nella Tecnica* (Milan: Edizione di Comunità, 1970), p. 180.

point for a study of English. Tarski, however, maintained that there could not be a theory of truth for English, because natural languages such as English are inconsistent, and so cannot have a consistent truth definition. He draws this surprising conclusion from the fact that any rules of truth adequate for English would have to allow for kinds of self-predication that are permitted in English, but which lead to paradox. Here is an example. The present sentence, the fourth sentence that begins on page 136 of this book, is false. The sentence you have just read is well formed in English but is false if it is true and true if it is false. There cannot be a consistent *T*-sentence corresponding to it. Paradoxes based on self-reference abound. Hence, said Tarski, there can be no consistent theory of truth for English as she is spoke.

Without denying the interest of these paradoxes Davidson suggests we should ignore them for the time being. Even if there is no consistent set of rules for the whole of English, we should expect a consistent set for almost all of it, excluding a few rather unimportant devices that allow for self-reference. This is a further example of Davidson's attitude already mentioned in subsection 1: we cannot do everything at once so let us get on with what is central, and see if we can construct a theory of truth for most of English.

3. *Tarski and the grammarians.* It is worth comparing the Tarskian need for a finite basis and the grammarians' quest, described earlier in Chapters 6 and 8, for a finite algorithm generating grammatical sentences. Chomsky claimed that there must exist a finite algorithm that will provide a formal model of a mental faculty used in acquiring and speaking our native tongue. Tarski made no use of such considerations about learning, but Davidson does so. Hence there are strong points of contact between Davidson's use of Tarski's theory and the programme of contemporary grammarians. But the two are not identical and we cannot now tell whether they will converge or diverge. Let us try to imagine some outcomes of these parallel lines of work.

It might turn out that the structures generated by a grammatical algorithm are the very ones needed to get a theory of truth running smoothly. But this might not happen. The influence of Tarski has been so strong that we now expect that the skeleton of any theory of truth will be first-order logic. Chomsky has been so influential that few grammarians think logic will solve their problems. These seemingly incompatible hunches are consistent. The original Chomsky programme aimed at a formal model of how we tell the grammatical from the non-grammatical. The Tarski theory of truth starts with a category of grammatical sentences and proves *T*-theorems for them. It would be pleasant if deep structure, in the sense of Chomsky, and logical form, in the sense of Russell (and adopted by Tarski) were to coincide, as suggested in Chapter 8. But that might not happen. Indeed only one of the programmes might succeed, while the other petered out. For example, *pace* Chomsky, it might prove impossible to construct an algorithm for English grammar simply because the way in which the human brain acquires a language is too complex for the human brain itself to conceptualize; yet a theory of truth for English, which took the recognition of grammatical sentences as given, might still be possible. Actually that is vastly unlikely. I mention this rather curious possibility only to insist that although there is much similarity in motivation and technique between the grammarians who have learned from Chomsky, and Davidson who follows Tarski, the differences between them might widen rather than (as we hope) diminish.

4. *The inadequacy of first-order logic.* First-order logic provides a good analysis of sentences using sentential connectives ('and', 'if . . . then', and the like), quantifiers ('all', 'some'), predicates (including relations), names, definite descriptions, and a good deal else. But if we are to follow Tarski and take first-order logic as the underlying structure for a truth definition in English, we shall have to extend it. One glaring omission is adverbs. A famous paper of David-

son's begins: 'Strange goings on! Jones did it slowly, deliberately, in the bathroom, with a knife, at midnight. What he did was butter a piece of toast.'[5] This reminds us that we can iterate adverbs almost indefinitely, and that we can draw deductive inferences from some adverbial modifications to others. For example, the following inference is certainly valid, and the validity depends on the form of the two sentences:

(i)   Jones is buttering toast with a knife, so,
(ii) Jones is buttering toast.

Unfortunately both *Principia Mathematica* and today's logic primers tell us that the logical form of the premise is 'Jones F's', where F stands for the predicate 'is-buttering-toast-with-a-knife', and the logical form of the conclusion is 'Jones G's, where G stands for the predicate 'is-buttering-toast'. Evidently the argument from 'Jones F's, so Jones G's' is not valid, but the above argument '(i), so (ii)', is valid. Hence this analysis is incomplete and fails to get at the logic of adverbial modification.

Davidson has attempted to construct a theory of adverbs as an extension of first-order logic. Note that any such extension will contribute to the study of truth. We may expect that a theory of truth will have an axiom giving the T-sentence for the simple 'He jumps.' But we do not want a further independent axiom for 'He jumps clumsily.' The T-sentence for the latter should be derivable from that for the former. Indeed it must be derivable, for there seems to be no end to possible adverbial modification of a sort that provides for such valid inferences. That is part of the point of that entertaining sentence about buttering in the bathroom. Our concern for a finite basis for a theory of truth forces us to an analysis of adverbs from which we will be able to prove the T-sentences for increasingly long strings of adverbs.

5. 'The Logical Form of Action Sentences', in *The Logic of Decision and Action*, ed. N. Rescher (Pittsburgh, Pa.: University of Pittsburgh Press, 1967), p. 81.

Notice that these considerations about adverbs, here motivated by semantics and logical theory, have strong repercussions on other branches of philosophy, notably the philosophy of mind and action. It is characteristically descriptions of actions that are modified by adverbs. So a theory on the logical form of action sentences leads to a theory of action itself. It also makes Davidson conclude that our language demands an irreducible category of *events*: we must admit into our ontology more, he claims, than *things* with varying *properties*. This is one of the many possible examples of the intersection of the seemingly divergent thrusts of Davidson's investigations. It illustrates one way that language can matter to today's philosophers.

5. *Logics of higher order.* Davidson wants to extend symbolic logic in a horizontal way, allowing for adverbs within a structure that is restricted to the first-order calculus that allows us to talk about individual things and their properties. Some logicians think the extension should be vertical, and that we should do higher-order logic. This would allow us to speak directly, and without analysis, of properties of properties, as when we say that red is a delightful colour. There are some profound technical results that have made many logicians leery of even second-order logic, which merely rises to properties of first-order properties. Owing to a certain completeness theorem that Kurt Gödel proved for first-order logic, but which does not hold for second-order logic, there is a strong sense in which we can be said to understand the semantics of first-order but not of second-order logic. But some workers, just as strongly influenced by Tarski as Davidson is, have found this no hindrance. Chief among these was Richard Montague. Shortly before his untimely death he developed a theory of universal grammar and semantics that makes essential use of a great deal of second-order apparatus.[6]

6. *Formal Philosophy: Selected Papers of Richard Montague*, ed. R. Thomason (New Haven, Conn.: Yale University Press, 1974).

Second-order logic is formally a more powerful device than any extension of first-order logic, and grammarians that employ it can claim a speedy analysis of many locutions of English that have not yet yielded to Davidsonian methods. But the penalty, according to Davidson, is high. At present the most popular way to provide an interpretation of second-order sentences is using the notion of classes of possible worlds. There is some immediate temptation to think this is a good move, for consider a sentence like 'Bertrand Russell might have lived to be 100.' What are the truth conditions for this? Some say the sentence is true if and only if there is some possible world in which that philosopher lived to be 100. Others, including Davidson, are bemused by such talk of possible worlds and wonder how one can identify our dead philosopher with someone alive in another possible world. Davidson is inclined to dismiss such moves with sarcasm:

There is even a danger that the know-nothings [who do not recognize that formal work in semantics is important to philosophy] and the experts will join forces; the former, hearing mutterings of possible worlds, trans-world lines, counterparts and the like, are apt to think, *now* semantics is getting somewhere – out of this world, anyway.[7]

The present situation is much more open than Davidson's remarks might suggest. We may be entering a decade dominated by Montague's 'Universal Grammar' with its semantics of possible worlds and its higher-order logics.

III. The theory of meaning

The sketch of a programme for truth has been only a preliminary. Meaning is our topic. One of Davidson's main ideas is as follows. A theory of truth for a language should enable me to understand any declarative sentence uttered by a speaker of that language. With a theory of truth I can translate everything he says, for if he utters *s* I know that what he says is

7. 'In Defense of Convention *T*', p. 78.

true if and only if *p*. So I can grasp what he is claiming to be true, if he is asserting *s*. Of course my theory may be wrong, that is, I may have an incorrect theory of truth for the language, but a theory of truth does enable me to interpret, rightly or wrongly, what a person is saying.

It seems to follow that a theory of truth is a theory of translation. Is it not thereby a theory of meaning? A theory of meaning is a theory of what is public, of what, according to Frege, is passed on from generation to generation. If a theory of truth, and of translation, provides me with a way to understand whatever is made public in language, it may then be a theory of meaning as well. Perhaps we might go so far as to take

(*T*) The sentence *s* is true if and only if *p*.

as the natural gloss or paraphrase of

(*M*) The sentence *s* means *p*.

We shall see that (*T*) by itself is a quite inadequate paraphrase of (*M*), but the idea here is important. In sections I and II we said a good deal about truth with hardly a whisper about meaning, and now it looks as if a theory of meaning will be delivered to us for free. That innocent biconditional, the 'true if and only if' of the *T*-sentence, seems transparent, whereas meaning has long seemed ineluctable and intractable. So it would be nice to swap *M* for *T*.

The nominalist streak in Davidson's philosophy lends further impetus towards the analysis of (*M*) by (*T*). When we say that some expression *e* means *m*, it may sound as if we are saying that the meaning of *e* is identical to the meaning of *m*, thereby postulating the existence of entities called meanings. Indeed it is clear that Frege thought of the *Sinn* (of an expression) as an object. What kind of entity is this? A nominalist philosopher like Davidson, always scared of multiplying entities beyond necessity, is relieved to discover that sameness of meaning can be explicated in terms of truth, and that *meanings* never need be mentioned at all.

There are virtues to the reduction of (M) to (T) additional to those perceived by latter-day nominalism. It provides an answer to another problem, namely 'of showing or explaining how the meaning of a sentence depends on the meanings of its parts'. There must be such a dependence, for how else could we learn a language with no upper bound on the number of possible sentences? A theory of truth, which must generate proofs of infinitely many T-sentences, shows how this is possible.

The slogan [that the meaning of the sentence depends on the meaning of its parts] reflects an important truth, one on which, I suggest, a theory of truth *confers* a clear content. That it does so without introducing meanings as entities is one of its rewarding qualities.[8]

Unfortunately the straightforward reduction of 'means' to 'is true if and only if' won't do. Since it is true, for example, that the sun rose yesterday, the following sentence is just as true as (1):

(5)   The German sentence 'Schnee ist weiss' is true if and only if the sun rose yesterday.

It would be wrong to replace 'is true if and only if' by 'means' in (5). What someone knew, if he knew (5), would be true, but he would not thereby be able to translate 'Schnee ist weiss.' Hence it is wrong to equate (T) and (M): we cannot blindly interchange 'is true if and only if' and 'means'.

The equation of (T) and (M) remains suggestive. A theory of truth demands not only true T-sentences; it requires that T-sentences be provable. Although (5) is a *true* T-sentence, it is not to be expected that a theory which proved only true T-sentences would enable us to *prove* (5). In comparing (T) and (M) we have ignored the requirement of provability. So it might be suggested that to know what a sentence s means is not merely to know a true T-sentence about s, but also to know the proof of it. This will surely exclude (5), for

8. *Ibid*. p. 81.

although (5) is true it is not the sort of thing to appear as a theorem.

Should we conclude, then, that to know the meaning of *s* is (i) to know a true *T*-sentence for *s* and (ii) to know the proof of that *T*-sentence? Well, perhaps if I had that much information about *s* I would know the meaning of *s*. But (i) and (ii) cannot be an analysis of the concept of meaning. For I know what lots of sentences mean, but know few enough proofs of *T*-sentences.

The mistaken identification of (*T*) and (*M*) remains alluring to a writer like Davidson who finds truth intelligible and meanings obscure. Thanks to Tarski we have the sketch of a rigorous theory of truth. Davidson wants to model a theory of meaning on the theory of truth. Ideally he would like a theory of truth to generate something very much like a theory of meaning but without employing any concepts foreign to the theory of truth. We tried doing this by identifying (*T*) and (*M*), but learned that the reduction of meaning to truth must be more circuitous if it is to work at all.

Let us take seriously the word 'theory' in 'theory of truth'. Think of more familiar experimentally controlled theories, such as the theory of electricity. We cannot just 'look' to see that it is correct. Nor can we even 'observe directly' that the electric potential (voltage) is in proportion to the product of the resistance and the current flowing through it. On the contrary the theory is an elaborate structure with a large number of, in themselves, trifling consequences that can be matched against our experience. Two factors are needed to make a theory compelling: it must impose a structure on a wide range of phenomena, and its low-level consequences must conform to whatever observations are possible. The requirement of structure corresponds to the Tarski demand that *T*-sentences be provable. The second requirement is simply that

If we consider any one *T*-sentence, this proposal requires only that if a true sentence is described as true, then its truth conditions are given by some true sentence. But when we consider the constraining need to match truth with truth throughout the language, we realize that any theory acceptable by this standard may yield, in effect, a usable translation manual moving from object language to metalanguage. The desired effect is standard in theory building: to extract a rich concept (here something reasonably close to translation) from thin little bits of evidence (here the truth values of sentences) by imposing a formal structure on enough bits. If we characterize the sentences by their form alone, as Tarski did, it is possible, using Tarski's methods, to define truth using no semantical concepts. If we treat *T*-sentences as verifiable, then a theory of truth shows how we can go from truth to something like meaning – enough like meaning so that if someone had a theory of a language verified only in the way I propose, he would be able to use the language in communication.[9]

'We can go from truth to something like meaning', says Davidson. The extra ingredient needed to effect this trick is that 'we regard *T*-sentences as verifiable'. How are we to verify *T*-sentences? Not piecemeal, but collecitvely, from 'thin little bits of evidence', and 'by imposing enough formal structure on the bits'. The formal structure to be imposed is a Tarski-type theory of truth. We have now heard a good deal about that. Exactly how do we come by the 'thin little bits of evidence' that constitute the other half of the corroboration of theory of truth?

IV. The verification of T-Sentences

Take any sentence of a foreign language that on some occasions of utterance is true and on others false. The German 'Es regnet' will do. The *T*-sentence should be

(6)   The German sentence 'Es regnet' is true if and only if it is raining.

In a fuller theory this would be amplified by mentioning the context or region in which it is said to be raining. What 'thin little bits of evidence' would lead us to (6)? There

9. *Ibid.* p. 84.

are plenty of kinds of evidence because we have ample commerce with Germans, but let us pretend we are engaged in what Quine calls radical translation, in which we confront this and other sentences of a thoroughly alien language from scratch. Then we have to rely on what speakers do and say in various situations. Some evidence for (6) might be this: 'Es regnet' is with regularity uttered only when it is in fact raining, by people who are in a position to know that fact, in contexts where some remark about the weather is apropos. All sorts of assumptions underlie any use we might make of this simple analysis. We first of all guess that the sentence s is used to express truth or falsehood. Then we suppose that by and large people utter it only when they think it is true, perhaps because they are trying to tell us something. Next we postulate that, at least for a large variety of commonplace situations, what they take to be true is more or less what we take to be true. Finally we notice that usually when they utter s it is true that p; when p is false they sometimes 'deny' s, or are put out, surprised, or amused when we tentatively say s. Moreover, even if candidates other than p come to mind, no q, r, etc. fit this bill quite so cleanly as p. In the light of all this, we find some verification for the conjecture that s is true if and only if p.

Each of these assumptions could be discussed at length. Many philosophers have urged that there *must* be devices of assertion and denial in a language, and that most of the time most people *must* be trying to tell the truth, and that communication *must* be the primary role of language. Most of the arguments seem to me to be pretty feeble. Many a traveller to foreign parts sometimes forms the distinct impression that the people whom he meets, thoroughly friendly and well intentioned, do not have the custom of conveying information. Language, in their community, seems to serve quite other ends, possibly more agreeable than that of communicating facts. Assumptions that philosophers will offer as necessary truths about language perhaps amount to no more than methodological advice which often is useful. Let us not pursue the point, but consider the additional assumption that so far as many humdrum matters are concerned, our foreigners usually have the same beliefs as we do. The assumption is clearly important, for if they are pretty often mistaken about the weather, the fact that they typically say 'Es regnet' when they can see it's raining is poor evidence that, in their language, 'Es regnet' is true if and only if it is raining. Perhaps the sentence is false if and only if it is raining and their weather lore, that they so confidently communicate to us, is all wrong! How are we to check up on the assumption that their beliefs are pretty well the same as ours? The question leads to several matters of importance, including a curious 'principle of charity'.

V. Charity and humanity

Before checking up on beliefs let us take a wider view. Beliefs and desires seem pretty distinct. I know what I like and I know what I think is true. I explain my actions by a combination of wants and beliefs. Why, you ask, did I choose that rotten melon? Because I prefer the taste of melons that are warm and fully ripe; the feel and the aroma of this melon made me think that it is delectable. When I cut it open it turned out to be completely rotten inside, but my mistake is readily explained by my desires and my beliefs. The modern discipline called decision theory provides a model of the interaction between wants and beliefs. It uses two scales and some mathematics to work out which actions are reasonable for me to undertake. One scale orders possible outcomes of action in terms of utility to me, and the other orders states of affairs by the probability that I attach to them. Probabilities measure degrees of belief and utilities display my preferences. Davidson carries this one philosophical step further. He says that desires and beliefs constitute not only the reasons for action but also the very causes of actions. Even if we do not go this deep into the analysis of human action or rational decision, we seldom confuse our wants and our beliefs. Things are not so simple when we contemplate the speech and behaviour of a complete stranger.

We see that the foreigner has picked a rotten melon and is dismayed when it is cut open. He may have been like me, thinking this was a pleasantly ripe fruit, and is someone who prefers melons that way, rather than the chilled green taste-less wedges often served up in restaurants. That is one explanation of his action and reaction. Perhaps, however, he thought that the melon was unripe, and likes to eat unripe melons. The hypothesis of masochism adds another twist to the possible combinations of belief and desire. Or maybe the man thought he had a cuckoo's egg and was hoping for an omelet. Or he is a diviner who thought that the state of the seeds in the melon would tell him who has been making free with his wife; he is shocked to discover that his own son is guilty.

If we speak the foreign language we can ask our man what he believed and what he wanted. But in radical translation from scratch his comments are open to many interpretations. He says that he believed *s* about the melon. Then *s* could mean 'This is a cuckoo's egg', and we attribute to him a pang for omelets. Or *s* could mean 'This melon is unripe' and we guess he wanted unripe fruit. In every case a reasonable guess at what he means will be a guess at two things: his beliefs and his wants. This is yet one more indication of why, although Davidson keeps his philosophy of mind and his phi-losophy of language fairly separate in his published papers, they constantly intersect in the substratum of his work.

We could let our imaginations run riot and attribute all sorts of beliefs and wants to our unhappy man with the rotten melon. We need at least a rule of thumb to suppress our romantic inclinations. Perhaps what N. L. Wilson calls 'the principle of charity' would help; it has certainly won wide-spread acceptance among armchair translators. He is considering the problem of a computer trying to find an interpretation for a corpus of sentences in a lost or alien tongue – he has Ventris' linear B in mind:

Not every corpus has a single *right* interpretation, right in the sense of being that interpretation under which the largest number of sentences of the corpus will be true. (What else could possibly make an interpretation 'right'?) The computer operates in accordance with what I have elsewhere called the Principle of Charity. It seeks that interpretation which, in the light of what it knows of the facts, will maximize truth among the sentences of the corpus.[10]

Wilson's rhetorical question 'What else could possibly make an interpretation "right"?' might well be answered in other ways. If the corpus expresses a lot of falsehoods, then, the uncharitable cynic will suggest, the interpretation that makes them all true can hardly be right. So the principle of charity is substantive: we are to assume that foreign beliefs are, in many commonplace matters, pretty much the same as our own. Our man may sometimes take a stone for a stick, and so may we, but we assume that in general most of our unspeculative beliefs are pretty widely shared. When it comes to speculation and theorizing there may be differences aplenty. In paternity suits we do odd things to blood samples that may seem sheer voodoo to the foreigner while his investigation of chicken guts to settle who begat whom may strike us as worthless. But at least at the level of 'That's a chicken' and 'Here's blood', we suppose in charity that our judgments usually coincide. The principle of charity is a methodological constraint on the kind of translations that we will tentatively admit.

Belief is perhaps too shallow a category on its own. We must guess that our stranger shares not only our beliefs but

10. 'Grice on Meaning: The Ultimate Counterexample', *Nous*, IV (1970), 300. Wilson coined the phrase 'principle of charity' in 'Substances without Substrata', *Review of Metaphysics*, XII (1959), 531.

also our interests. The presence of chicken livers in the soup may, we guess, prompt conversation about offal, while a clear night in which Venus dominates the western sky may arouse interest in the Evening Star. But if our pointing at the planet induced a discussion of livers while the organs of hens got him started on astronomy, then we might never get on, even if on both occasions we both strove desperately to tell the truth. For this reason, and because of the more general way in which belief and desire are interlaced when it comes to the description of action, Richard Grandy urges more than charity:

It is of fundamental importance to make the interrelations between [the other person's beliefs and desires] as similar as possible to our own. If a translation tells us that the other person's beliefs and desires are connected in a way that is too bizarre for us to make sense of, then the translation is useless for our purposes. So we have, as a pragmatic constraint on translation, the condition that the imputed pattern of relations among beliefs, desires and the world be as similar to our own as possible. This principle I shall call the *principle of humanity*.[11]

The very names given to these principles, and the fact that some writers invoke them as principles to enable us to translate the speech of 'natives', may raise a wry smile. 'Charity' and 'humanity' have long been in the missionary vanguard of colonizing Commerce. Our 'native' may be wondering whether philosophical B52s and strategic hamlets are in the offing if he won't sit up and speak like the English. Linguistic imperialism is better armed than the military for perhaps it can be proved, by a transcendental argument, that if the native does not share most of our beliefs and wants, he is just not engaged in human discourse, and is at best sub-human. (The native has heard that one before too.)

There is of course nothing wrong with the principles of charity and humanity if they are just commonsense rules of

11. 'Reference, Meaning and Belief', *The Journal of Philosophy*, LXX (1973), 443.

thumb that might, like all common sense, sometimes offer bad advice. The 'principle of charity' is often attributed to Quine, but it is not really his, and, as he engagingly says,

The maxim of translation underlying all this is that assertions startlingly false on the face of them are likely to turn on hidden differences of language . . . The common sense behind the maxim is that one's interlocutor's silliness, beyond a certain point, is less likely than bad translation.[12]

VI. The determinacy of translation

On their voyage of discovery to Australia a group of Captain Cook's sailors captured a young kangaroo and brought the strange creature back on board their ship. No one knew what it was, so some men were sent ashore to ask the natives. When the sailors returned they told their mates, 'It's a kangaroo.' Many years later it was discovered that when the aborigines said 'kangaroo' they were not in fact naming the animal, but replying to their questioners, 'What did you say?'[13]

This splendid tale about the origin of the English word 'kangaroo' reminds us that even if we were to exercise all the charity, humanity, and good will in the world, radical translation could, for a time, go hopelessly awry. Further commerce between peoples would, we hope, eliminate such gross mistakes. But let us consider what, in principle, are the possible outcomes of long-standing 'friendly collaboration' between two linguistic groups. We know the actual outcome all over the globe. Except when adventurers have eliminated natives, quite satisfactory systems of translation have been devised, and indeed they are, aside from a few hilarious counter-examples, fairly transitive. That is to say, a translation from language E into language F, and then from F to language G, and then from G back into E, recaptures a good deal of what was originally said in E. The greater the cultural gap between

12. *Word and Object* (New York: M.I.T. and Wiley, 1960), p. 59.
13. *The Observer* (London), magazine supplement for 25 November 1973.

two civilizations the more the nuances that get lost, but most peoples do communicate a good deal with relative ease. This has not prevented philosophers from composing more romantic stories of what could happen.

There are three philosophical fantasies that we could label 'too much', 'too little', and 'just right'. The just-righters are closest to reality, for they claim there is just one right system of translation between any pair of languages. I think that Davidson's theory of meaning obliges him to be a just-righter. Philosophical debates currently focus on the claim that there is *too much* free play between languages to determine any uniquely best system of translation. The most famous exponent of this is Quine, who calls it the indeterminacy of translation. Imagine that we observed all there is to observe about speakers of an alien language. We know every occasion on which any sentence was, is, or will be uttered, and we know all the observable precedents and consequences of each such occasion. We even know how speakers of that language are disposed to talk in situations they never in fact experience. In short, we know infinitely more than any radical translator ever could know. Even if we knew all that, there are, claims Quine, indefinitely many mutually incompatible systems of translation that would square with the data. This is a strong claim, for two systems are incompatible if a sentence *s* is said by one to mean *p*, and by another to mean *q*, yet *p* can be true when *q* is false, or, better, *p* and *q* are actually contraries.

In *Word and Object* Quine has given a good many different kinds of argument for his thesis. He does not claim that every sentence is up for multiple translation. Some sentences have what he calls 'stimulus meaning'. For example, the sentence 'This is orange', first uttered in the presence of an outstandingly visible orange orange, may turn out to be regularly matched with physiological events in the eye. In general it is imagined by Quine that some such sentences can be correlated with stimuli presented to sense organs whose functioning is shared by the entire human species. This correlation furnishes interlinguistic stimulus meaning. Quine takes for granted that 'retinal' stimulation is what counts, and that 'ocular irradiation patterns' are the things to study. It is seldom noticed that this conception of the eye as the chief organ of primary knowledge is peculiar to the positivist European world that emerged in the eighteenth century, and that even in Europe, let alone the rest of the world, vision had other roles in some conceptual schemes before that time. If it were true, as Lucien Febvre claims (cf. p. 32 above), that proto-French is almost entirely auditory and olfactory in its classifications, then Quine's study of stimuli by what he calls 'properly timed blindfoldings' of Gauls might have yielded unexpected results.

Utterances with something close to stimulus meaning have, says Quine, a unique translation and hence there is little indeterminacy at the level of reports of observation. This limitation on possible translation acts at the lowest and most humdrum level of conversation. Quine also admits a constraint acting from the top. Good sense (or charity) inclines us to exclude any system of translation that would lead us to infer that the natives assert brief and obvious self-contradictions. But although these constraints acting from top and bottom squash some sort of order into possible translation manuals, Quine contends that there can be an indefinitely large range of mutually incompatible systems of translation consistent with all possible behavioural data.

Quine urges that there is *too much* possibility for translation. The opposed doctrine maintains there is *too little*. Two human languages could be so disparate that no system of translation is possible. This is in the spirit of Feyerabend's doctrine of incommensurability. He wrote about competing or successive scientific theories, but we can extend this point of view to independent language systems. To say that there is no system of translation between languages E and F is not to say that F is impenetrable to speakers of E. But the E people can learn F only in the childish way of learning mostly from scratch. After they have done so they realize that a preponderance of sentences of F (if indeed F has 'sentences' at all) have no expression in E. It is not just that individual words fail us, but that sentences, paragraphs, wondering, fears, questions, and jokes expressed in E cannot be represented in F. Perhaps F does not even have wonderings, fears, or even jokes, just as English has no *tawahura* or *jok*.

Languages, like incommensurable scientific theories, can on this view be learned from inside by a man of good will but they do not necessarily lend themselves to translation. Peter Winch is one English philosopher who has developed such a thesis, partly by elaborating some remarks of Wittgenstein, and partly by engaging in debates that currently vex social science.[14] Some of the greatest anthropological pioneers write as if they *experience* this incommensurability. The problem has long been discussed, both in practical and theoretical terms, in German philosophy of the human sciences (often under the heading of *Verstehen* 'understanding' or 'comprehension'). Every sustained discussion of these matters should go back to the analyses proffered by Max Weber, which in turn are brought into being by, among others, Wilhelm Dilthey (1833–1911). Their scope on the surface is a good deal wider than questions about translation, for one is concerned with the entire range of human experiences and possible ways of understanding or explaining it.

Davidson's theory of truth and meaning is inevitably at odds with both incommensurability and indeterminacy. If most domains of discourse in some language contain lots of sentences with no true T-sentences, translation into our language via a Tarski theory of truth is not going to be much help in explicating meaning in the other language. So evidently Davidsion is obliged to confute much of the incom-

14. *The Idea of a Social Science and Its Relation to Philosophy* (London: Routledge and Kegan Paul, 1958).

mensurability thesis. On the other hand, he is lukewarm about the indeterminacy thesis. He thinks that in order to understand a language at all, one must do something tantamount to translating it by a Tarski theory. It seems that this is possible only if we can find, in the other language, structures of first-order logic used in the proofs of T-sentences. So every language, if it is to be counted a language at all, will have an underlying logic identical to our own, and this will immensely limit the admissible translations. Indeterminacy will enter chiefly at the level of predicates. There cannot be two translations of a sentence, one of the form S is P, and the other not in subject–predicate form. But there might be nothing to choose between two schemes of translation, one rendering a sentence S is P, and another assigning S is P^* to the same sentence, even though P and P^* are contraries. Here, on Davidson's view, is where indeterminacy enters.

Although Davidson does allow that there can be indeterminacy of this sort, I think he should not do so. He ought, I think, to be even more of a 'just-righter'. For suppose, with Quine, that there are in principle too many translations. Then there will exist, for the preponderance of sentences s of L, a translation 's means p' in one system of translation and a translation 's means q' in another. There will be nothing to choose between systems, but p and q may be contraries. Now recall that for Davidson such statements of translation must match with T-sentences. So there will be nothing to choose between a T-sentence 's is true if and only if p', provided in one system, and 's is true if and only if q', provided in another system. Yet we had the initial overriding requirement that T-sentences are true. Since p and q may be contraries, *both* T-sentences cannot be true. From Davidson's standpoint, this is a *reductio ad absurdum* of indeterminacy.

Davidson can readily agree that quirks and nuances of one language may not always be exactly and uniquely expressed in another. There will be divergent systems of classifying things, and theoretical concepts will have developed in one culture that cannot be made present to another without, in a sense, converting it to new theories. The difficulty lies with a systematic pervading Quinean excess or Feyerabendian shortage of translation manuals. To get a theory of meaning out of a theory of truth, Davidson must, I contend, require that there be just one systematic system of translation, even if it is loose or ambiguous on small points of nuance. It must however be adequate and unequivocal on topics that touch most of our daily life. Indeterminacy and incommensurability both deny that there must be any such manual. He has recently denounced incommensurability in public, but on the topic of indeterminacy he is, thus far, more reserved.

Several ideas of his can, however, be made out. He believes that some of Quine's indeterminacy arises from too simplistic a view of theory construction. According to Quine there are sentences that have stimulus meaning; these play a role like that of 'observation sentence' in empiricist philosophy of science. They constitute the only given, and a theory can latch on to these in any consistent way that it can. Quine writes as if theories are unhistorical, timeless. But, insists Davidson, they are historical and constructed and tested over the course of time by those 'thin little bits of evidence'. No one has been more vehement in opposing any sharp dichotomy between theory and observation than Quine, and yet it is as if, in reflection about language, he forgets his own strictures. Davidson thinks that when we attend to the different kinds of ways in which linguistic evidence can intersect with theoretical structure, the slack for which Quine argues largely disappears. Then enters Davidson's *credo*, that any theory of language must be a (horizontal extension of a) first-order theory of truth. Such a theory has so much structure in it that, when combined with the need to match classifications of ordinary things in daily life, there simply will not be mutually incompatible theories. As for the other evil, of sheer incommensurability, Davidson thinks that students of Feyerabend pay too much attention to theoretical concepts, such as mass, or fields of force. At a lower level of generality there must, Davidson contends, be an immense amount of agreement about chickens and blades of grass and what's wet and whether a camel hair goes through the eye of a needle. And once there is translatability of simple sentences in which these occur, then the recursive generation of truth conditions for more complex sentences will enforce such a uniform method of translation that the spectres of incommensurability and indeterminacy will vanish in the dawn of a thoroughly worked out theory of truth. We shall have a theory of meaning that insists on truth but does not postulate a special class of entities called meanings.

13. Why does language matter to philosophy?

The dozen philosophers who have been made to play their parts upon our stage would all answer this question in different ways. There are lots of reasons why language has mattered to philosophy, and the reasons have doubtless been different in the several eras of philosophical speculation. Sometimes concern with language has obsessed philosophers to the point where deep matters were too little touched upon. In other periods failure to reflect at length upon the nature of language has perhaps done harm. No one can doubt that language has mattered to many philosophers. I have chosen my topics with a particular tradition in mind, and within that tradition I have allowed free play for my own tastes. Even so we have had a good gamut of traditional Great Problems: truth, reality, existence, logic, knowledge, necessity, dreams, ideas. Another choice, even within the same tradition, might have given us chapters on God, freedom, morality, induction, intention. Had we used a quite different kind of net, we should have pulled in plenty of philosophico-linguistic reflection on society, history, consciousness, action, and Man.

Aside from what, in the opening chapter of strategy, I called the minor reasons why language has persistently mattered to philosophers, there need not be any true and interesting general answer to my question. Indeed, I am sure that no such answer is valid over the whole domain of Western philosophizing from Plato to the present. There need not even be a general answer to the question of why language matters to philosophy today. Even if there were a true and general answer, we should not win immediate agreement. So I invite every reader to speculate as he will, considering the examples that I have used and the philosophers whom he has read. In this chapter I take the opportunity to join that discussion.

It is time to take an overall view of our case studies. They come in three groups: the heyday of ideas, the heyday of meanings, and the heyday of sentences. The relations between these three will teach us something about why language matters to philosophy. The connections that I wish to portray are complex, but my account will be simple, almost banal. It is possible to dress it up in fancy clothes but it is better to begin with a stripped-down synopsis. This will both serve as a signpost through the occasionally tortuous elaborations to follow, and also help fend off any delusions about the intellectual depth of the analysis.

What is the connection between the period of which we take Locke or Berkeley as typical, and that represented here by Feyerabend or Davidson? On the one hand we contemplate a finished object, namely the seventeenth-century philosophizing I call the heyday of ideas. We may disagree about how to describe it but we know what it is and readily locate its more distinctive features. On the other hand we experience an open and ongoing activity that we call contemporary philosophy. We do not yet know for sure what is notable about it. But although it is hazardous to compare the two I shall claim that they have the same structure but different content.

This weighty talk of structure and content will be cheerfully caricatured by two diagrams, one for the old era, one for the new. In one figure a number of 'nodes' are related in what are, formally, the same manner as the nodes in the other, but the elements in the nodes are different. So we say that the two diagrams have the same structure and different content. 'Ideas' do not even exist today, yet Port Royal could say as quoted on p. 28 above: 'Some words are so clear that they cannot be explained by others, for none are more clear and more simple. "Idea" is such a word.' We still have the word but nothing of this character answers to it. I shall claim that the fundamental seventeenth-century node occupied by ideas is nowadays taken over by the sentence.

Ideas were once the objects of all philosophizing, and were the link between the Cartesian *ego* and the world external to it. Connections between ideas were expressed in mental discourse, and formed representations of reality in response to changes in the ego's experience and reflection. In today's discussion, public discourse has replaced mental discourse. An unquestioned ingredient of all public discourse is the sentence. If it were not for a few technical niceties, philosophers nowadays would say about 'sentence' what Port Royal once said about 'ideas', that the word is too simple for definition. The sentence is the simple object taken as fundamental in the explanation of truth, meaning, experiment, and reality. Quine has said that 'the lore of our fathers is a fabric of sentences'. The sentences in this fabric of public discourse are an artefact of the knowing subject. Perhaps, as I shall soon suggest, they actually constitute this 'knowing subject'. At any rate, they are responsible for the representation of reality in a body of knowledge. So sentences appear to have replaced ideas.

Once one node changes, all the rest go too. We illustrated this in Chapter 3, showing how the mutation that got rid of 'ideas' also shifted our understanding of 'object' and even of 'vision'. If something seemingly as immediate as vision can be dislocated, then my bland place-holders such as 'reality', 'experience,' and even 'the knowing subject' cannot be expected to persist without distortion. We say that the structure of the seventeenth-century situation is isomorphic to our own, but we should take seriously the contention that content has changed. It is not just a local transition from ideas to sentences that we must note, but a radical transformation in our modes of understanding.

Further features of the transformation will be indicated in my comments on particular periods. Before attempting to describe the other aspects that have changed, we ought to begin with some gross conjecture about the causes of change. I think that knowledge itself must be the primary force that drives the transformation from the heyday of ideas to the heyday of sentences. Knowledge is not what it used to be. We know more than our predecessors and we conceptualize knowledge differently, but that is not what I mean. The very nature of knowledge has changed. Our present situation in philosophy is a consequence of what knowledge has become.

What has it become? 'The lore of our fathers' – so runs Quine's aphorism – 'is a fabric of sentences.' Knowledge, says Quine, is constituted by interrelations. He may be right. Our lore, and the lore even of our fathers, is a fabric of sentences. But the lore of our ancestors was not. Knowledge has not always been essentially sentential.

To say that knowledge has become sentential is to restate rather than explain the emergence of the heyday of sentences. To avoid such tautology one wants to say that knowledge has become theoretical. Alas, that observation is equivocal because the very word 'theory' has adapted its connotations to the evolving nature of knowledge. An historical dictionary tells us that the word used to mean speculation or contemplation. Chasing down the temporal sequence of evolving sub-definitions we find: 'A scheme or system of ideas or statements held as an explanation or account of a group of facts or phenomena'. Quotations illustrating this usage of the word 'theory' begin in 1638 and run to the present. What a fine portmanteau! A Descartes would no more have thought a theory to be a system of *statements* than a Quine would acknowledge that a theory is a scheme of seventeenth-century *ideas*.

Today's philosophers of science teach us that a theory is a system of statements or sentences. The doctrine is crystallized in the classic analysis of scientific explanation that we owe to

C. G. Hempel.[1] When I say that knowledge has become theoretical I mean 'theoretical' in this sense of the word. It will be noticed how in the course of our case studies this usage was increasingly taken for granted until with Davidson and Feyerabend no other meaning is even contemplated. So it is not very informative to say that knowledge has become theoretical. We still mean primarily that it has become sentential.

The claim that the nature of knowledge has changed is in double jeopardy. Some readers will find it so trite that it is not worth while characterizing how knowledge has changed. Other readers, of a more conservative philosophical demeanour, will find it so paradoxical that no amount of clarification will be persuasive. How can the literal truth of our claim be proven? Philosophers themselves provide *prima facie* evidence. The account of knowledge provided by an Aristotle, an Aquinas, or a Descartes is radically different from anything on show today. Nothing in their discourse even means 'knowledge'. Before the scientific revolution the best words seem to be *scientia* and *episteme*. They had to do with knowledge demonstrated from first principles, and they involved knowledge of causes of things derived from acquaintance with essences.

The earlier lack of a word for our 'knowledge' does suggest that something happened in and after the seventeenth century. But can we conclude that the new knowledge was sentential while the old *scientia* was not? It will be protested that if science used to be *demonstration* from first *principles*, then it was surely sentential. For what, it will be asked, is a principle but a sentence, and what is a mathematical demonstration but a sequence of sentences? How words deceive us when we forget their etymology, that is, when we forget what they once

1. C. G. Hempel and Paul Oppenheim, 'Studies in the Logic of Explanation', *Philosophy of Science*, xv (1948), 135-75; reprinted with other works on explanation in C. G. Hempel, *Aspects of Scientific Explanation and Other Essays in the Philosophy of Science* (New York: Free Press; London: Collier–Macmillan, 1965).

meant! A demonstration used to be a showing: a showing to the eye, the only eye, the inward eye. That which was shown was the principle: namely the origin, the source. The source was the essence, that which made the object what it is. Knowledge which is acquaintance with essences has little in common with the arrangement of sentences. Leibniz was the first philosopher of our era to understand that mathematical proof is a matter of form, not content, constituted by formal relations within a sequence of sentences. Thus, although Euclid and Archimedes had provided the model of rigour for millennia, the notion that their discoveries are sentential first appears in the seventeenth century. Despite the genius of Leibniz it was not publicly accepted until the beginning of the twentieth. Descartes taught the older way of contemplating proof. Proof is a device to remove the scales from our eyes, and the thing to do with proofs is not to check the formal steps slowly and piecemeal, but to run over the proof faster and faster until the whole thing is in one's head at once, and clear perception is guaranteed.

Once upon a time the philosophers did not think that knowledge is a matter of sentences – not even in the most favoured case of Euclidean or Archimedean theorems. Our modern philosophers of science tell us that all knowledge is sentential. Such a change in philosophical opinion is not conclusive – perhaps one or the other school of philosophy was simply mistaken. Perhaps Aristotle was just wrong about essences or Quine is just wrong about sentences. Let us not take up such issues too seriously. This is no place to settle what Greek science 'really' was. To express the matter in the least controversial way we can see that the nature of knowledge has changed sufficiently that totally different emphases have been appropriate in different epochs. Aristotle's account of the knowledge of his time is plausible, imaginative, important, and explanatory. If we try to turn it into a universal analysis of modern knowledge, it loses all those virtues.

Granted that philosophers' theories of knowledge have

altered radically, has knowledge itself changed? Hardly any of us have mastered more than the elements of kinetic theory, Marxist historiography, biometrics, electromagnetism, or even Keynesian economics. So one may ask whether the knowledge of 'ordinary people' is different in kind from that of their ancestors. In reply it is possible to invoke N. R. Hanson's opinion, cited in Chapter 11, that most of our terms of common speech are actually 'theory-laden'. But that is off the point. The philosophy of know-nothings is no philosophy. Serious philosophy has always wanted to be in Locke's phrase, at least, an 'underlabourer' to the best speculative and creative thought of the time. The heyday of ideas began in self-conscious awareness of the new knowledge of the seventeenth century. The new kind of knowledge, which brought the philosophy of ideas in its wake, was the very force that in the end transformed the heyday of ideas into the heyday of sentences. In the next few sections we shall have to make specific observations about this or that heyday, and it will be easy to forget the global view of what drives the whole thing along. So bear in mind that it may be nothing less than an evolution in the nature of knowledge itself.

A. The heyday of ideas

My illustrations of this era ran from Hobbes' *Leviathan* of 1651 to Berkeley's *Principles* of 1710. There is no doubt that ideas were once paramount in philosophy. So powerful was their sway that it made little sense even to ask what an idea is. Ideas persisted long after Berkeley. I have regularly spoken of them as peculiar to the seventeenth century, but this mode of reference is an artefact of our decimal dating system. Everyone knows that ideas mattered a good deal to Hume (1711–76). 'The way of ideas' was systematically denounced not as a particular mistake but as a general kind of error by the Scottish philosopher of common sense, Thomas Reid (1710–96). But if we were historians we should have to note the endurance of ideas in the work of Locke's French successors. We would trace a continuous path through Condillac (1715–80) and Condorcet (1743–94) to the group that became known as *idéologues*. Its founder, Destutt de Tracy (1754–1836), began by coining the name *idéologiste* for members of his school. Although we find many variations on 'idea', there is a stubborn strand of continuity throughout, marked by the regular appearance of 'philosophical' or 'universal' grammars. The end was nigh with Destutt de Tracy's *Grammaire générale* of 1803, for in that year, ideology (in the sense of that movement) was officially abolished. It had briefly dominated the select Class II of the *Institut National* in Paris, the section for 'moral and political science'. It was second only to Class I for 'mathematical and physical science' (actually embracing most of the natural sciences). Napoleon reorganized Class II out of existence in 1802–3, sarcastically proclaiming that the verbose *idéologues* were irrelevant to the new French state. Ideology, in the sense of Destutt de Tracy – which might have been the sense of Locke – was stone dead by the time Marx came to write *The German Ideology*. The very word 'ideology', which, like 'idealism' before it, had denoted a doctrine of seventeenth-century 'ideas', came, at the hands of Marx and others, to mean what we mean by it today. The way of ideas is sufficiently antique that it lends itself readily to diagrams. Fig. 1 is the very simplest of models.

The expression 'mental discourse' on the right of the diamond belongs to Hobbes. I call the *ego* Cartesian, while the terms 'experience' and 'reality' are used in some sort of modern sense, and would not have come readily in the heyday of ideas. Nevertheless the structure displayed in Fig. 1 neatly encapsulates an era in the history of philosophy. The question marks in the arrow from Ideas to Reality and from Reality to Experience, indicate the problem area of Locke or Berkeley. Experience acts upon the *ego* to produce ideas that are ideas of reality, that in turn cause experience. Locke will

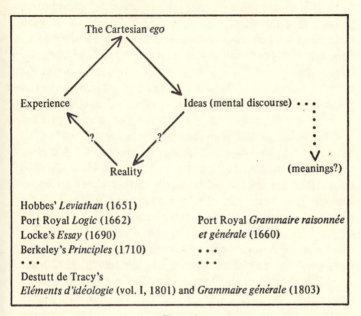

The Cartesian *ego*

Experience

Ideas (mental discourse) · · ·

? ?

Reality

(meanings?)

Hobbes' *Leviathan* (1651)
Port Royal *Logic* (1662)
Locke's *Essay* (1690)
Berkeley's *Principles* (1710)
· · ·
Destutt de Tracy's
Eléments d'idéologie (vol. I, 1801) and *Grammaire générale* (1803)

Port Royal *Grammaire raisonnée
et générale* (1660)

· · ·
· · ·

Figure 1

insist that we have a quadrilateral firmly linked to a reality
that is external to mind. Berkeley will collapse this figure by
making reality identical to mind. Arnauld and Malebranche
tell other stories. Leibniz, who often fought to return to an
older position, was indifferent to ideas and found such problems boring. He did metaphysics and methodology, while the
new way of ideas engaged in, and indeed identified, what we
now call metaphysics and epistemology.

It is an anachronism to speak of epistemology here. If one
consults any good modern outline of epistemology one will
find a survey starting with the Pre-Socratics. But the dictionary gives 1854 as the first use of the word 'epistemology' in
English; *Erkenntnistheorie* entered German about the same

time. It is in the spirit of many theses underlying the present chapter that the word was invented only when there was a separate discipline for it to denote. Although we shall find it convenient to count the heyday of meaning as beginning with Frege twenty years later, we might do better to argue that meanings are an early stage in the entirely new discipline calling itself epistemology. The 'theory of knowledge' was not an identifiable discipline in the heyday of ideas, precisely because ideology, although reacting to the new kind of knowledge then evolving, was still trying to understand it in a piecemeal way in terms of its entry into the mind. Hence, the old books that are used nowadays in lecture courses on epistemology bear titles like 'Essay Concerning Human Understanding'. Epistemology so-called begins when it becomes recognized that knowledge is public, and is not merely a mode of existence of 'human nature', 'understanding', or 'reason'. Epistemology needs an object; its object is knowledge; knowledge was not conceived of as an autonomous object until quite recently. Symptoms of this fact are everywhere. For example the British Association for the Advancement of Science was founded in 1831 'to obtain a more general attention to the objects of Science'. In its volumes of that time one finds the special sciences beginning to be recognized as objects with their own institutions. The thinker who had been called philosopher, or natural philosopher, began to be styled, e.g., physicist (a word coined in 1843 by the greatest of ninteenth-century philosophers of science, William Whewell). The emergence of a named study of autonomous knowledge – epistemology – coincides with the differentiation and naming of kinds of knowers, e.g., physicists.

In presenting the heyday of ideas in Chapters 2 to 5, I harped on the negative theme that in those days no one cared about meanings. By meanings I meant what Frege called *Sinn*, objects whose existence he postulated to explain the common store of human thoughts transmitted from generation to generation. If we look at Fig. 1 we see no central place for public meanings, so my argument may have seemed unnecessary. It was directed specifically against philosophers from the period that I call the heyday of meanings, who have recently read seventeenth-century discussions as a collection of theories of meaning that contributed to the overall philosophy of the time. The best textual evidence for such an interpretation is seldom stated; the programmes of general grammar that serve to define the heyday of ideas from Port Royal to Destutt de Tracy certainly suggest that meanings mattered. But general grammar, as we have seen, was the grammar of mental discourse. The grammar of actual languages was to be explained and analysed in terms of an underlying grammar of the mind. Fregean *Sinn*, if it is to be found at all, is suspended from a little hook at the far right of mental discourse, and is peripheral to the existing problem situation.

I have not emphasized the absence of meanings in order to provoke a quarrel with some recent commentators. The absence is in itself a clue towards the understanding of some subsequent phenomena. In particular we find that empirically oriented philosophers in the heyday of meanings take for granted that their British predecessors were concerned with the same problems as vex us nowadays, and moreover that old solutions to these problems were conditioned by mistaken theories about meanings. It is usually a harmless anachronism to call Locke an epistemologist, but why commit the more substantive error of attributing theories of meaning to the seventeenth century?

There are three possible answers. (1) I am wrong; meanings constitute a central theme in the work of a Locke or a Berkeley. (2) The recent commentaries are wrong, and the old problems are not the same as ours. (3) My own answer: the structure of the recent philosophical problem situation, especially as conceived by the large number of workers who write in English, is formally identical to the seventeenth-century one, but the content of that structure is different. Schematically, we still have a quadrilateral as Fig. 1, but the nodes bear different labels. Public discourse replaces mental discourse, and the sentence has, in our time, replaced the idea as something so clear that it does not require explanation by anything else, because nothing else is 'more clear or more simple'. So we are taught that much of the 'confused' treatment of idea is really a discussion about meanings.

Any answer to the question Why does language matter to philosophy? ought to explain what is right and what is wrong in these recent readings of the seventeenth century. That is a virtue of the present analysis. The commentators, I claim, correctly discern the similarity of the old problem situation to our own. Then they apply the principles of charity and humanity, stated in Chapter 12.V above. It would be uncharitable, and indeed inhumane, if they did not interpret the greatest minds of the seventeenth century as discussing the problem in what are now known to be the right ways. So the old texts, which say almost nothing about public discourse, must *really* be talking about meanings! Exegesis of this sort is a version of the biblical criticism called hermeneutics. The hermeneuticist tries to re-experience the ancient words in terms of his own life and problems, thereby uncovering the profound and hidden meanings that lie beneath the text. It will be noted that serious philosophy of hermeneutics – in the writings of Wilhelm Dilthey (1833–1911) – is coeval with the heyday of meanings. Writing as I do in the heyday of the sentence I reverse the procedure of hermeneutics, charity, or humanity, and read only what is written on the surface, for there is nothing else.

We are about to repeat the absurd leap already perpetrated in Chapter 6, from the heyday of ideas to the heyday of meanings – without even touching the backs of Kant, Hegel, and the bulk of modern philosophy. Before doing so it is worth noticing what, within the heyday of ideas, came to seem the weakest point on the quadrilateral drawn in Fig. 1. It is the very starting point, the Cartesian *ego* itself. No one seems to have reduced the *ego* to contradiction before Hume.

He did so only in an honest but embarrassed Appendix to Part III of his *Treatise*, published in 1740, a year after Parts I and II had been printed. In two pages he demolishes his entire system.

Upon a more strict review of the section concerning *personal identity* [*Treatise* I.iv.vi], I find myself involved in such a labyrinth, that, I must confess, I neither know how to correct my former opinions, nor how to render them consistent.

Hume taught that every idea must have an antecedent impression. His book is based on a theory about the origin of ideas. So, by way of afterthought he is driven to ask, what is the impression from which we form the idea of the *self*, without which none of the rest makes much sense?

There are two principles, which I cannot render consistent; nor is it in my power to renounce either of them, viz. *that all our distinct perceptions are distinct existences*, and *that the mind never perceives any real connection between distinct existences.*

Hume would like to say that our idea of the self is complex, combining successive states of consciousness. But what is the principle of combination that uniquely defines the ineluctable *ego*? My perceptions are distinct existences if for no other reason than that they occur at different times. On Hume's principles there is no way to perceive a common factor between items that are distinct, so there is no perception of what my perceptions have in common. The mind has, therefore, no way to bundle up states of consciousness to form an idea of its self. We began with the Cartesian *ego* and then, by rigorous application of empiricism to the world of ideas, finally splintered it into myriad shards that can never be conjoined.

Once Hume had written, his countryman Thomas Reid was ready to tell us at length that the entire way of ideas was on the rocks. More profound analysis was called for. Philosophy cried out for a doctrine of the 'transcendental unity of apperception', which is to say a theory according to which the oneness of different states of consciousness is prior to, and a necessary condition of, any judgment whatsoever. Kant provided it with his 'Transcendental Deduction of the Pure Concepts of the Understanding' in the *Critique of Pure Reason*.

B. The heyday of meanings

By now we know which work on ideas to call classical. The study of meanings is too recent for that. If present trends of interpretation or canonization within our tradition continue, then Frege will have an honorific place. Perhaps we shall deem that he inaugurated an era of philosophizing, just as we find it convenient to regard Port Royal as the herald of ideas. With the exception of Frege nothing else about meanings has established itself as manifestly classical. If, contrary to my own opinion, we are still living through the heyday of meanings then some basic texts are not yet written. So I make no special claims for the works described in Chapters 6 to 10. Plenty of other examples would have served as well to illustrate recurring themes and shifting problems. The selections provide some suggestions about how to analyse the whole period, but they are not adequate for any firm induction.

The somewhat haphazard character of the case studies, and the lack of agreed classical texts, form only one ground for not attempting an overview. Far more important is the fact that what I call the heyday of meanings is only a tiny part of a much vaster heyday that spans most aspects of the intellectual life of the era. Frege nicely isolates the beginning of a certain tradition of analysis that has been popular with Anglo-American analytical philosophers. He does more than that: we used him to characterize that meaning of 'meaning' that we were going to focus on. Frege said that there had to be *Sinn* because there was a common stock of knowledge transmitted from generation to generation. The sentences would not do; there had to be meanings beneath the sentences that are understood and are the actual bearers of belief and knowledge. Meanings make public discourse possible. In the present book we followed Frege and understood a theory of meaning to be a theory about the possibility of public discourse.

Frege is only a slice from the plum-filled cake of meaning on which his contemporaries gorged themselves. If we took a wider survey, we might be surprised to find that the title (though not the content) of his paper *Uber Sinn und Bedeutung* was almost trendy. Everyone was writing about kinds of meaning and using all the words available in the language in which they wrote to mark out the meanings of meaning. A passing reference to some of the success stories is in order. By reflecting on the problems of interpretation of historical texts, Wilhelm Dilthey fabricated a philosophy of history founded almost entirely on concepts of meaning. His work made hermeneutics an important theoretical science. Max Weber constructed his general theory of sociology from an analysis of meaning. Turn to his *Economy and Society: An Outline of Interpretive Sociology*, Volume I, Part I, Chapter 1, section A, subsection 1 ('Methodological foundations') and we start:

'Meaning' may be of two kinds. The term may refer first to the actual existing meaning in the given concrete case of a particular actor, or to the average of approximate meaning attributable to a given plurality of actors; or secondly, to the theoretically conceived *pure type* of subjective meaning attributed to the hypothetical actor or actors in a given type of action.

The word used for 'meaning' was none other than *Sinn*. It is one of the same words that Dilthey employed, and that Edmund Husserl used in his attempt to understand the meaning of the direct insights that we have in the course of mathematical reflection, and also of the content of our immediate perceptions. This is the foundation of phenomenology. We say nothing of the explosive theories of meaning that animated literature and the arts. It is no wonder that by 1923 C. K. Ogden and I. A. Richards could separate sixteen fundamental meanings of 'meaning' in their book, *The Meaning of Meaning*.

Anyone who recognizes the utterly provincial character of

what, in the present book, serves as the heyday of meanings will see that it is idiotic to present any very general theses on the basis of our insular data. The preconditions for the great heyday of meanings that swamped European culture require more profound analysis than anything attempted here. So we shall not strive for the lustre of generality.

Meanings are important enough within the framework of our case studies. Chapters 7 and 8, whose heroes are Russell and Wittgenstein, show a little speculative philosophy in which meanings matter. Chapters 9 and 10 present two stages of verification, and display some critical philosophy that is even more concerned with the presence and absence of meanings. Chapter 6, on the old and new innatism, reminds us of a strand that runs back to Port Royal and on to tomorrow: there the problem is not about the meanings of words but about how meanings arise from the structure of sentences. This particular preoccupation is also manifest in Chapter 8 where we treated the problem of articulation as it arises in the *Tractatus*. We can all agree that meanings have played an exceptional role in this type of philosophical work and that reflections on meaning have been put to all sorts of purposes. This is not the only immediate moral. There have also been changes of interest. Russell illustrates this quite clearly.

It is to some extent an accident of longevity that makes us group Russell with the other thinkers we have studied. He may represent an earlier age. Meanings do not matter to him in the same way that they do in the little bit of Wittgenstein's *Tractatus* to which we alluded, or in the two stages of verificationism illustrated by Ayer and Malcolm. The study of meanings, for these other writers, is at the heart of philosophy, while for Russell it is chiefly prophylactic. More than almost any of those predecessors that reach back to Socrates and beyond, Russell thinks that it is crucial to have a very clear analysis of language. But although his emphasis is different, his motive is the time-honoured one. Wrong notions about language, or defects in our language, betray us into bad philosophy. A better and more analytic language is needed to encode the truth, but true philosophy is not the servant of grammar or theory of meaning. On the contrary, far from being autonomous and perhaps even constituting the substance of ontology (as some of our contemporaries appear to believe) Russell always thought that grammar answers to the world and to what there is in it.

For example, only if Stalin and Bismarck are indeed ultimate individuals can a logical grammar admit proper names that purport to stand for such people. The grammar of English may build into itself the prephilosophical view that the world is full of unanalysed persons, and it may make us uncritical of our beliefs. It can contribute to vicious conservation of former superstitions. 'The influence of language on philosophy has' – so we quoted him on page 70 above – 'been profound and almost unrecognized.' Liberation, he thought, requires a good theory of language and of its logical form. But philosophy is an attempt to understand the world, the given. Russell never believed that the answer to or abolition of a philosophical problem could be relegated entirely to reflection on language.

Subsequent philosophers made a theory of meanings more than prophylactic. Hence in our time Frege is more revered than Russell. On page 70 above we repeated Russell's remarks that 'A logically perfect language . . . would be very largely private to one speaker' and 'It would be absolutely fatal if people meant the same things by their words.' We might call that a theory of anti-*Sinn*: communication gets along because we do not mean the same things by our words! Russell's well-known hostility to the new linguistic philosophy is no trifling matter of generation gap. It is a gulf between conceptual schemes, between a point of view that thinks that all language is essentially private, and a point of view that thinks no language can be essentially private.

Wittgenstein said early in his career that the limits of language are the limits of my world. Russell might have judged that to be a witty turn of phrase or even an instructive meta-phor but he could never think that thought literally, as Witt-genstein did. When we turn to read Ayer or Malcolm we find that criteria of meaningfulness are used to settle what can be true of the world. There is a paper in which Ayer disproves the immortality of the soul by reflecting on the meaning of statements expressing personal identity.[2] Russell believed that as a matter of fact he is mortal. Hence, the joke in which he is portrayed at the Last Judgment, pleading, 'Lord, you did not give us enough evidence. We could not know.' God, who is a Scottish Presbyterian, retorts, 'Well, ye ken noo!' and consigns him to hellfire. On Ayer's analysis that cannot happen to *Ayer*, although it will happen to someone strikingly similar. In the heyday of meanings we think that we can settle substantive philosophical issues by contemplating meanings. This leads to the new kind of philosophical idealism that, to avoid the solecism inherent in the word 'idea', might better be called lingualism.

Wittgenstein is the dominant figure in the heyday of mean-ings but his relation to it is equivocal. In my pages he is an *éminence grise*, a shadowy figure often alluded to but seldom present. Failure to describe his work is no loss. There are plenty of first-rate new and forthcoming books about him. One reason for keeping him in the background was stated in our chapter on strategy: his work is very difficult. It arouses strong passions. Its explication demands whole books. I wanted to leave aside both the difficulties and the dangers. Even in the discussion of Wittgenstein's 'objects' we stuck to the subsidiary theme of the structure of the sentence and never entered the philosophy proper.

One curious feature of Wittgenstein's work is persistent: influence and divergence. We see it at the beginning, in his interaction with Russell. Russell's philosophy of logical atom-ism owes its inspiration to conversations with Wittgenstein

2. *The Concept of a Person* (London: Macmillan, 1963), pp. 115f.

prior to 1914. Yet the philosophy that emerged has almost nothing in common with Wittgenstein's, a fact that the latter felt strongly when he read Russell's Introduction to the *Tractatus*. The very 'atoms' of the two men were incommensurable. Russell's were sense-data and universals, the former existing only for fleeting instants. Wittgenstein's were something else and appear to be outside the temporal scheme altogether.

This pattern of influence and divergence endures throughout Wittgenstein's life work. Tales of the Vienna Circle are full of portraits of a brooding Wittgenstein casting a spell over the assembled company. The verification principle often was associated with his name. Yet in no form in which it was advanced by the men of Vienna did it hold any charms for him. His explanation of the nature of logical truth as tautology did solve some problems for the Circle, yet his motivation was altogether different from the features that made his theory attractive to that group. Here we have a second example of philosophers acknowledging profound debts to Wittgenstein yet following a path that he found alien.

Passing to a later period, Norman Malcolm, in the brief and personal biography *Ludwig Wittgenstein: A Memoir*, describes the impact of his teacher with wisdom and candour, but the impartial reader must concede that the key motifs in Malcolm's work, although plainly taken from Wittgenstein, are developed to very different ends. Or, to take a more stark example, Wittgenstein is much remembered for his motto, 'Do not ask for the meaning, ask for the use.' A whole generation of philosophers took this seriously and wrote at length on the usage of words. It rather looks, however, as if they did so in order to determine the meanings of the words they used. Perhaps this is not quite what Wittgenstein intended!

The relationship between Wittgenstein and philosophy written in English is problematic. It is unlikely to be well understood for some time. Some readers may care to put together a few well-known facts. First, it is commonly said that Wittgenstein alone has given the world an historical succession of two well-elaborated systems and methods of philosophy. Secondly, we know that British philosophy was moribund from Hume to Russell; no matter how much we fancy Reid or Mill or Whewell, there is no Kant, Hegel, Marx, Schopenhauer, Nietzsche. Thirdly, we notice that among the plethora of books about Wittgenstein now in progress we find some valuable studies illustrating how Kantian themes are developed, first in the *Tractatus*,[3] and then, in the *Philosophical Investigations*.[4] We shall shortly have essays 'Wittgenstein and Schopenhauer' and 'Wittgenstein and Nietzsche'. Finally, we note that for the first time in two centuries there is a real and growing coincidence between the problems, though not the idioms, of some of the more important elements of anglophone and Continental philosophy. It is as if the travail of the German philosophers, which the English and Americans were never able to endure, was abstracted by this troubled man who was never at home in either culture. He took our philosophy hurriedly across many of the painful transformations that had been worked out elsewhere.

Such a model makes it possible to understand the regular pattern of influence and divergence that we have mentioned, but it would be disagreeable to elaborate this thought and thereby accelerate the process of turning the person L. W. into an anonymous figure in the history of ideas. If there were some truth in this kind of model, then the jump from the heyday of ideas to the heyday of meanings may, though quick, not be quite so unhistorical as on the surface it appears. It also suggests that although one could try to identify the lifetime of Wittgenstein as the heyday of meanings, we should follow his own broader teaching and regard that heyday as ephemeral. As he said, don't ask for the meaning.

3. Erik Stenius, *Wittgenstein's Tractatus* (Oxford: Blackwell, 1960).
4. P. M. S. Hacker, *Insight and Illusion: Wittgenstein on the Philosophy and the Metaphysics of Experience* (Oxford: University Press, 1972).

C. The heyday of sentences

Doubts about meanings began to appear in the course of Chapters 6 to 10. The verification principle started boldly telling us what has meaning but it ended with a sorry footnote to Hempel's article 'The Empiricist Criterion of Meaning'. He was quoted on page 101 above, hoping that anything meaningful can be translated into an 'empirically pure' language, but admitting that 'The notion of translatability needed in this context is by no means fully clear, and an attempt to explicate it faces considerable difficulties.'

The next generation of verificationism was represented in Chapter 10 by Malcolm's solution to a problem about dreaming. It petered out in a dispute with Putnam. Malcolm claimed that when we study nocturnal behaviour we may discover new criteria for telling when someone is dreaming, and thereby change the meaning of the verb 'to dream'. Putnam protested that meanings remain unchanged; we just find out more about dreaming. We might hope that subsequent studies of this kind of disagreement would have settled the matter but instead we only get inconclusive chapters often called 'The Problem of Meaning Variance'.

The examples of Chapter 9 and 10 illustrate how doubts about meanings often begin as by-products of an enquiry that has little to do with semantics. Quine, the most notable critic of meanings, is a case in point. Because his own vigorous expositions are so readily available and because so much has already been written about them elsewhere, I have not attempted a detailed account of his opinions. We should note, however, that they did not start from the pure theory of meaning but from traditional debates about the nature of mathematical truth. Frege had asserted that arithmetic is analytic, i.e., deducible from definitions and general laws of logic. Wittgenstein contended that the laws of logic are degenerate by-products of our notation. The Vienna Circle combined these two doctrines, saying that all mathematical truth is a consequence of facts about language, in short, is true by convention. Quine began in 1935 challenging truth by convention and later pointed to general difficulties in any notion of analyticity.[5] Fregean analyticity, he claimed, could be explained in terms of synonymy, and synonymy in terms of analyticity, but neither term can be characterized independently. This is a miserable little circle with which to explain the very nature of mathematics. He then advanced to a more general critique of meanings, including the theory of the indeterminacy of translation discussed above in Chapter 12. vi[6]

Meanings, Quine implies, are a hoax. All we need are sentences and their interrelations. I have often quoted his aphorism to the effect that knowledge is a fabric of sentences. It is worth noting that it occurs at the end of a criticism of Carnap's version of conventionalist theory of mathematical truth: the fabric of sentences is pale grey, 'black with fact and white with convention. But I have found no substantial reasons for concluding that there are any quite black threads in it, or any white ones.'[7] The drive from meanings to sentences, although now a general thrust in much philosophical writing, is, as here, usually commenced with a specific application to a problem of philosophy rather than from reflection on meaning in the abstract.

The Feyerabend of Chapter 11, is, in style and temperament, an altogether different philosopher from Quine. Casual dipping into the essays of each would suggest that they came from unconnected traditions. That would be a mistake. Both want to revise a version of positivism. Quine started with the Vienna Circle, and Feyerabend with the Copenhagen school

---

5. 'Truth by Convention', reprinted in W. v. O. Quine, *The Ways of Paradox and Other Essays* (New York: Random House, 1966).
6. The position culminates in *Word and Object*. The most notable stage in the journey is 'Two Dogmas of Empiricism' (1951), reprinted in W. v. O. Quine, *From a Logical Point of View* (Cambridge, Mass.: Harvard University Press, 1953).
7. From the final paragraph of: 'Carnap and Logical Truth', in *The Philosophy of Rudolf Carnap*, ed. P. A. Schilpp (La Salle, Ill.: Open Court, 1963); reprinted in Quine, *The Ways of Paradox*.

of quantum mechanics. Both the Circle and the school have been called children of Ernst Mach; if so, the philosophies of Feyerabend and Quine must be his grandchildren. Both Feyerabend and Quine object to elements of positivist methodology but both make a similar positivist move away from meanings towards sentences. Thus we saw that Feyerabend denies that a crucial experiment will be able to decide between radically competing theories, on the ground that no statement, no agreed 'meaning', can be available to adherents of different sects trying to express the observed outcome of an experiment deciding between them. The 'only way in which experience judges a general cosmological point of view', we quoted him on page 127, is when it 'causes the observer to carry out certain actions, for example, to utter sentences of a certain kind'. It is not the 'observation statements' made by the experimenter that report on the decision between theories, but the sentences complete in themselves, not tricked out with meanings.

Quine told us that translation is too easy, for there are too many translations between languages or theories for 'sameness of meaning' to have any bite. Knowledge consists in the fabric of sentences itself, not in what those sentences mean. Feyerabend reaches a parallel conclusion from the opposite direction. Translation, he teaches, is too hard, and one must master the theory as it stands, not translate it into another. Davidson, it may appear, strikes the balance between these two extremes. In a calm and measured tone he tells us that both panic stories are mistaken. In English one often says that so and so means such and such, that 'patricide' means a person who kills his or her father. How absurd to suppose that there is no sameness of meaning! Davidson revives meaning by proposing a theory of translation located in a theory of truth. Meaning will never be mentioned; we get along fine with sentences and their truth conditions. So we are led right back to the Quine–Feyerabend supremacy of the sentence. Davidson resuscitates meaning by administering the kiss of death.

There are plenty of other pointers in the same direction. We could for example have investigated Wittgenstein's so-called 'private language argument' which seems to show that there cannot be a private language. Public discourse is primary. It is, of course, no part of the argument that a particular instrument of public discourse, the sentence, is what matters. It is however central that no meaning that can be directly apprehended prior to discourse can constitute the sense of a sentence.

Despite all these indications, one cannot confidently announce the death of meaning, when at the very time that I gave this book in lectures there appeared Michael Dummett's long-awaited opus, *Frege: Philosophy of Language*. The literary weeklies justifiably hail this as the most important work of philosophy to have appeared for some time. We are offered, among other things of greater consequence, a Frege who has learned all there is to learn from Quine and who has mastered much of what can be gleaned from Wittgenstein. Meaning, it seems, lives.

Nor ought one to declare the death of meaning when the investigations of H. P. Grice have not yet matured. Three established philosophers have most attracted the interest of research students I have encountered in recent years: Feyerabend, Davidson, and Grice. So, in addition to the chapters of Feyerabend's *theories* and Davidson's *truth*, I had hoped to write about Grice's *intentions*. Like the other two philosophers, Grice has given only scattered papers and an inviting programme. Some references are given in the bibliography for Chapter 13. I found I could not pull it together well enough to write a satisfying chapter. Grice offers a model of what a person may mean by what he does. The core of the analysis lies in the intentions of the agent to affect witnesses to the action. The action may be speech. The meanings of sentences, Grice says, are derivative on what a person means, and have to do with certain conventional ways in which intentions may be expressed. There are a good many points of coincidence between Grice and the doctrines that I have recently discussed, but this must not conceal the fact that the orientation of his programme is radically different. Far from the sentence being paramount, its meaning is to be explained more generally in terms of action. Far from public discourse being the sole repository of communication, it is to be explained in terms of the intentions of speakers and the beliefs of hearers. It is true that these mental entities are given a strong behaviourist tinge. But as I hinted in Chapter 2, and have subsequently confirmed, there is much in common between Grice's investigations and Hobbes' view of language. With work like this in the offing it would be foolish to go on arguing from examples that meaning is dead. Only a theory explaining why (*pace* Grice and Dummett) the sentence and its kin are dominating philosophy will carry any conviction.

My own conjecture is already given in my synopsis: knowledge itself has become sentential. The diagram that corresponds to Fig. 1 must be something like Fig. 2.

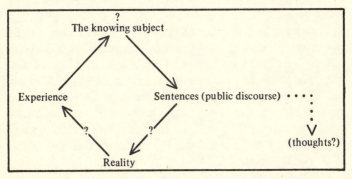

Figure 2

It is by now of no moment whether *sentence* is quite the kind of entity that we want at the rightmost node. What matters is that it is some linguistic entity, a text or discourse perhaps, regarded as an object in itself and not merely as the bearer of some antecedent meaning. I have amply emphasized that when one node changes, all of the others change, so most of the other tags are inadequate too, particularly, as I shall show, that dubious 'knowing subject'.

Although the content of the philosophical problem situation may change, it is important that certain formal moves are preserved. Take the most blatant example, the Berkeley who is said to have short-circuited Fig. 1 by making reality mental. We call that idealism. There is a corresponding short-circuit to Fig. 2. Parallel to idea-lism is a linguistic idealism or lingua-lism, which makes all reality linguistic. Wittgenstein said early that the limits of his language are the limits of his world. I know of no reputed philosopher who has advocated lingua-lism at length, seriously maintaining that all reality is verbal. It is of course only an extreme reading of Berkeley which makes us attribute even to him the view that all reality is ideal, so it is not surprising if we can find no one of comparable stature who will sport the label of lingualism. But symptoms of incipient lingua-lism are common enough.

For example, recall Berkeley's opinion that to be is to be perceived, *esse* is *percipi*. When one argues against a Berkeley (as Hylas against Philonous in the *Three Dialogues*) that plenty of existents are unperceived, one is asked for an example. One says, the tree behind our backs, or whatever, and he replies, but you have just made present to me an idea of that tree. I grant existence to it, he continues, but I also perceive (in Berkeley's sense of the word) the idea of that tree, so this is no counter-example.

I have had an exactly parallel conversation with a gifted student trained in both German and English traditions. Finding him inclined to say that something is real only insofar as it enters into communication, I have protested: there are polar bears on Baffin Land that no one has ever spoken about. His reply: you are speaking about them now, and any counter-example you adduce will have to be communicated to me, so my opinion is unvanquished!

As I have said, there is no widely admired statement of a lingualism as extreme as this. Sometimes, however, we find that agents with other ends in view enact in pantomime the birth or death of a philosophical doctrine. We have noted that Napoleon formally abolished idea-ology. George III, though sometimes said to be crazy, was no idea-list, but Richard Nixon has lived lingua-lism. The doctrine of lingualism is that only the sentence is real. Nixon preserved all the sentences uttered in his presence because they were the reality compared to which all else is passing show. Journalists and judges have complained that occasionally an uncomprehending secretary has cut this or that bit of tape; thereby they miss the truly fantastic fact that the President chose to end his career rather than burn his tapes. He destroyed himself rather than destroy the reality, the sentences. The gang known as White House plumbers burgled some and probably many houses leaving untouched all that sane men count as valuables, seeking only to steal the sentences of the other, in a vain hope of possessing their reality. A monstrous parody of philosophy has been acted out on the stage of a madman.

Idealism and lingualism are infinite excesses whose possibility we must note but whose content is seldom discussed with profit. The top node in our diagram is more interesting than the bottom one. I have called it 'the knowing subject' and matched it against the Cartesian *ego*. What is it? I recalled that Hume ended his *Treatise* by admitting a contradiction in the idea of the self, which he could not resolve. P. F. Strawson's important Kantian books *Individuals* and *The Bounds of Sense* offer a sort of sentential version of Kant's Transcendental Unity of Apperception, the theory by which Kant sought to resolve Hume's contradiction. If I am right about what has driven philosophy from the heyday of ideas to the heyday of sentences, then Strawson must be engaged in inadequate half-measures. Although the pronoun regularly

occurring in his work is 'we' rather than *ego*, he appears to be
investigating the conditions that must be satisfied for a bunch
of egos to enter into communication and share a scheme of
concepts similar to 'ours'. The transition from the singular to
the plural is more radical than that because the fabric of sentences is essentially public – to the extent that no single
person can even think of mastering its entirety. Fig. 2 is
almost certainly an anachronism, an anachronism shared by
Strawson, Quine, and other individualists, in which our state
of knowledge is still mapped on to the philosophical position
of the nascent bourgeoisie of the seventeenth century. Knowledge, once possessed by individuals, is now the property of
corporations.

This anachronism leads us, for the first time, to regret the
insular account of philosophy provided in this book. We have
not yet begun to conceptualize that topmost node, 'the knowing subject' or perhaps to contemplate removing it altogether.
Alone of notable philosophers who now work in English the
point is urged by Karl Popper. He has tried to work out what
he calls 'Epistemology without a knowing subject'.[8] What
Popper calls 'objective knowledge' is literally a fabric of sentences: 'Examples of objective knowledge are theories published in journals and books and stored in libraries; discussions of such theories; difficulties or problems pointed out in
connection with such theories; and so on.'[9] With his characteristic brilliantly simple statement of a complex situation he
continues, 'We can call the physical world, "world 1", the
world of our conscious experiences "world 2", and the world
of the logical *contents* of books, libraries and computer memories, and such like "world 3".' He says moreover that there
is a sense in which this third world is *autonomous*: the word
and its emphasis are his. Perhaps the core of Popper's philosophy is the short-circuiting of world 2: he sees epistemology

8. *Objective Knowledge: An Evolutionary Approach* (Oxford: University Press, 1972), ch. 3.
9. *Ibid.* p. 73.

as constituted by the ways in which world 1 and world 3 interact. World 3 is a product of mankind, and most of our corporate products of a more physical sort could not be fabricated without the third world.

I have compared a few of the ways in which the seventeenth-century doctrine of ideas matches that of the sentence. The names of historical personages from different eras could not possibly pair off exactly: Berkeley is without peer. But Popper's rendering of the sentence autonomous does resemble what Spinoza did to ideas. Ideas, in the work of Spinoza, are items of consciousness for individual men and women only in the derivative way that Popper's third-world sentences belong to the people who first uttered them. In Spinoza's time, ideas were just like sentences nowadays, the interface between the knower and the known. Spinoza and Popper appear to transform this dichotomy in parallel ways by making the interface the very nature of knowledge. According to Spinoza, the world of ideas is autonomous, while Popper grants similar autonomy to the world of the sentence. Popper's enquiries seem to me much more important than many of those that I have described in this book. I have said almost nothing of his work, partly because it is so closely interwoven with that embarrassing gap between the heyday of ideas and the heyday of sentences, the lacuna marked by another philosopher sometimes compared to Spinoza: Hegel.

The French Marxist philosopher Louis Althusser defines the 'principal *positive* debt [of Marx, and by implication, all of us] to Hegel: the concept of a *process without a subject*'.[10] Alone of major figures who now work in English, Popper grapples with this legacy of Hegel. Although he has written the most brilliant theoretical rejection of the Hegelian mode of thought that he calls 'historicism', he alone is there to teach us something about the basic Hegelian lesson from

10. 'Marx's Relation to Hegel', *Politics and History: Montesquieu, Rousseau, Hegel and Marx* (London: New Left Books, 1972), p. 185.

which Popper takes his title 'Epistemology without a knowing subject'.

The title of Popper's book, *Objective Knowledge*, serves as well as any as the name of his third world, the world of knowledge that is autonomous, the world which, although a product of human endeavour, has its own existence and perhaps its own laws. The subtitle, *An Evolutionary Approach*, may be more suspect. Popper rejects my thesis that knowledge itself has changed. He rejects it with argument and evidence. He grants that hardly any philosophers self-consciously acknowledge the world of the sentence, but that is a defect in philosophers that he traces systematically back to Plato. But he finds a number of happy formulations of an almost-grasping of the idea, even in the writing of Francis Bacon and Galileo. It is possible that my thesis is merely part of the present fad for rupture and revolution in recounting the history of science. But I do not think the change in the nature of knowledge is merely a matter of degree. At the most humdrum level, the 'books, libraries and computer memories', in which Popper says Objective Knowledge now resides, either did not exist, or had only a marginal existence until fairly recently. Galileo's character Simplicio, so Popper reminds us, 'is made to say that in order to understand Aristotle one must keep every saying of his always before the mind'. That recalls Descartes' proposal to get the entire proof of a theorem in one's mind all at once. It is no mere matter of degree that a man of sufficient genius once could get all his proofs in his head and also all the sayings of Aristotle. Objective Knowledge is no longer at all like that, and that may be precisely why Objective Knowledge is now autonomous of world 2. Evidently I have no quarrel with students of technology like Marshall McLuhan who think that the so-called scientific revolution of the seventeenth century is only a spin-off from the invention of printing, and who forecast comparable mutations when the locus of the sentence passes from the book to the computer printout via the technology of semiconductors.

The recognition of an essentially sentential autonomous knowledge brings with it new objects of enquiry, new domains of investigation. We can try to find out what transformations occur in the fabric of sentences. One can begin, with Althusser's former student Michel Foucault, to postulate 'anonymous' discourses existing at various times and places, individuated not by what they mean, but by what is actually said, in all its specificity, in certain sites, under the aegis of various institutions. One can enquire whether the conditions which make a discourse possible are those that determine the possibilities of what can be said within a discourse. We can reflect on how our own sentences participate in some present discourse, not as our own, but rather as cut off from we who speak, and autonomous and anonymous, like all discourse. The methodology of such enquiries has only just begun, and perhaps quite different routes to these investigations will be more profitable than any I could cite.

At any rate, I have one answer to the question of why language matters to philosophy now. *It matters for the reason that ideas mattered in seventeenth-century philosophy,* because ideas then, and sentences now, serve as the interface between the knowing subject and what is known. The sentence matters even more if we begin to dispense with the fiction of a knowing subject, and regard discourse as autonomous. Language matters to philosophy because of what knowledge has become. The topics of this or that school, of 'linguistic philosophy', 'structuralism', or whatever, will prove ephemeral and will appear as some of the brief recent episodes by which discourse itself has tried to recognize the historical situation in which it finds itself, no longer merely a tool by which experiences are shared, no longer even the interface between the knower and the known, but as that which constitutes human knowledge.

Bibliography

References in the text to standard works by Locke, Hobbes, etc. give volume, chapter, and section where possible, in order that any of the many available editions can be consulted. The best library reference book on philosophers and their work is Paul Edwards' eight-volume *Encyclopedia of Philosophy*.

Chapter 1 Strategy

I say little about some of the most widely read works of linguistic philosophy, because they can now be obtained so readily. Many of the most typical examples first appeared in journals but are now collected in anthologies such as:

> Richard Rorty, *The Linguistic Turn: Recent Essays in Philosophic Method*, Chicago: University of Chicago Press, 1967.
>
> Charles E. Caton, *Philosophy and Ordinary Language*, Urbana: University of Illinois Press, 1963.
>
> J. M. E. Moravcsik, *Logic and Philosophy for Linguists*, The Hague and Paris: Mouton, 1975.

Perhaps J. L. Austin (1911–60) is the quintessential philosopher of language. His work survives in a volume of papers and two posthumously edited small books of lectures:

> *Philosophical Papers,* Oxford: University Press, 1961.
>
> *How to Do Things with Words*, Cambridge, Mass.: Harvard University Press and Oxford: University Press, 1962.
>
> *Sense and Sensibilia*, Oxford: University Press, 1962.

The movement owes much to G. E. Moore (1873–1958), whose work is well represented by:

> *Philosophical Papers*, London: George Allen and Unwin and New York: Macmillan, 1959.

His 1936 paper 'Is Existence a Predicate,' no. vi in this collection, is a superb early example of the application of purely grammatical data to traditional metaphysics. Ludwig Wittgenstein

(1889–1951) is the most memorable figure of all. The first pair of books are his major works, but many readers find one or the other of the other pair an easier way into his work:

Tractatus Logico-Philosophicus, trans. D. F. Pears and B. F. McGuinness; London: Routledge and Kegan Paul and New York: Humanities Press, 1961.

Philosophical Investigations, trans. G. E. M. Anscombe, Oxford: Blackwell, 1953.

The Blue and the Brown Books, Oxford: Blackwell, 1958.

On Certainty, ed. G. E. M. Anscombe and G. H. von Wright, trans. Denis Paul and G. E. M. Anscombe, Oxford: Blackwell, 1969.

Chapter 2 Hobbes

The library edition of Hobbes is Molesworth's eleven-volume *The English Works of Thomas Hobbes.* There are plenty of editions of *Leviathan,* but other philosophical works are less easy to come by. All my quotations are in:

Hobbes: Selections, ed. F. J. E. Woodbridge, New York: Scribner's, 1930, 1958.

My emphasis that Hobbes' 'signification' has less to do with meaning than cause-and-effect leads to an account of Hobbes at variance with accounts such as those in:

Richard Peters, *Hobbes,* Harmondsworth: Penguin, 1956.

J. W. N. Watkins, *Hobbes' System of Ideas,* London: Hutchinson, 1965.

There is a recent scholarly article with an emphasis similar to mine:

Isabel C. Hungerford and George C. Vick, 'Hobbes' Theory of Signification', *Journal of the History of Philosophy,* XI (1973), 459–82.

These authors attribute widespread misreading of Hobbes to mistranslation, and say that Hobbes, who did his most careful work in Latin, was rather indifferent to English versions of his work, even when he wrote or approved them himself. They are preparing a new and accurate translation.

Chapter 3 Port Royal

As indicated by the quotation in this chapter, many readers have been puzzled by the notion of 'idea' in Locke, Berkeley, and Hume. It has recently been argued that there is a consistent set of seventeenth-century senses of the word, which we can disentangle without any serious conceptual rethinking:

Stephen L. Nathanson, 'Locke's Theory of Ideas', *Journal of
the History of Philosophy,* XI (1973), 29–42.

If more radical rethinking is necessary, the Port Royal *Logic; or
the Art of Thinking* is a natural place to start. There are several
cheap French editions of the Port Royal *Logic.* The only current
English translation has only Antoine Arnauld on the title page,
although the usual attribution is to Arnauld and Pierre Nicole.

The Art of Thinking: Port Royal Logic, trans. James Dickoff
and Patricia James, Indianapolis, Ind.: Bobbs–Merrill, 1964.

There are two recent important discussions of the linguistic theories stemming from Port Royal. Neither is run-of-the-mill philosophy, but, although each paints a different picture, both help
convey the background:

Noam Chomsky, *Cartesian Linguistics: A Chapter in the History of Rationalist Thought,* New York: Harper and Row,
1966.

Michel Foucault, *The Order of Things,* London: Tavistock,
1970, Ch. IV (originally published as *Les Mots et les choses,*
Paris: Gallimard, 1966).

The former, the work of the notable linguist, is chiefly directed at
linguistic theories evidenced by Port Royal and its successors,
while the latter, the major work of a contemporary French epistemologist, is concerned with a larger part of the existing system
of knowledge. In preparing these chapters I have been much
influenced by Foucault's work, but most people find it very hard
to follow. The following two books of his have a narrower range
of subject matter and thus may be easier to grasp. Both have the
same overriding theme as *The Order of Things.* The former is
about changing conceptions of madness, the latter about transformations in the practice of medicine and the conception of illness.

Madness and Civilization, London: Tavistock, 1967 (*Histoire
de la folie,* Paris: Plon, 1961).

The Birth of the Clinic, London: Tavistock, 1973 (*Naissance
de la clinique,* Paris: Presses Universitaires de France,
1963).

Chapter 4   Berkeley

The Principles of Human Knowledge, published when Berkeley
was twenty-five, is the chief source of his philosophy, and a
highly readable one. My comments have dwelt on his Introduction to this work. The body of the book is largely taken up with
questions about perception. *Three Dialogues between Hylas*

and Philonous is intended as a more popular version of the doctrines of the *Principles*, but once again is more explicitly concerned with perception than language. Two commentaries and an anthology with different emphases are:

G. Warnock, *Berkeley*, Harmondsworth: Penguin, 1953.

J. F. Bennett, *Locke, Berkeley, Hume: Central Themes*, Oxford: University Press, 1971.

C. B. Martin and David Armstrong, *Locke and Berkeley*, Notre Dame, Ind.: University of Notre Dame Press, 1968.

Chapter 5 Meaning

Bennett's book just cited is the clearest statement in disagreement with the present chapter. One of the 'central themes' of his title is *meaning*, whereas I contend that Locke and Berkeley had no theory of meaning. Bennett's opinion is supported in the vast majority of recent works on British empiricists.

Chapter 6 Chomsky

The classic debate about innate ideas is located in:

John Locke, *An Essay Concerning Human Understanding*, Book I.

G. W. Leibniz, *New Essays Concerning Human Understanding*, Preface and Book I, trans. A. W. Langley, Chicago: Open Court, 1916.

The translation of the latter is hard to come by. There is a paperback of the original French: Paris: Garnier Flammarion, 1966. The Locke–Leibniz controversy comes at the end of a century of vivid debate involving many issues. For some of these see:

Robert McRae, 'Innate Ideas', *Cartesian Studies*, ed. R. J. Butler, Oxford: Blackwell, 1972.

This author very much doubts the historical accuracy of Chomsky's account of early linguistics and innatism in *Cartesian Linguistics*, cited already for Chapter 3 above. Chomsky's two best-known books on language are:

Syntactic Structures, The Hague: Mouton, 1957.

Aspects of the Theory of Syntax, Cambridge, Mass.: M.I.T. 1965.

His philosophical views about language are argued in:

Language and Mind, New York: Harcourt Brace and World, 1968.

The best elementary survey of Chomsky's work is:

John Lyons, *Chomsky*, London: Fontana, 1970.

Chapter 7 Russell

The most convenient collection of Russell's papers bearing on the topics of this chapter is the one cited as *LK* in the text:

> *Logic and Knowledge*, ed. R. Marsh, London: Allen and Unwin, 1956.

There are now several surveys of Russell's work. Ayer's is brief, lucid, and lively.

> A. J. Ayer, *Russell*, London: Fontana, 1973.
>
> David Pears, *Bertrand Russell and the British Tradition in Philosophy*, London: Fontana, 1967.
>
> Ronald Jager, *The Philosophy of Bertrand Russell*, London: Macmillan, 1972.

Chapter 8 Wittgenstein

This chapter makes no attempt to give an overview of the *Tractatus*. The following secondary sources may be consulted; the last-mentioned gives a word-by-word analysis and concordance to Wittgenstein's book.

> G. E. M. Anscombe, *An Introduction to Wittgenstein's Tractatus*, London: Hutchinson, 1959, 1971.
>
> Erik Stenius, *Wittgenstein's 'Tractatus'*, Oxford: Blackwell, 1960.
>
> James Griffin, *Wittgenstein's Logical Atomism*, Oxford: University Press, 1964.
>
> Max Black, *A Companion to Wittgenstein's Tractatus*, Cambridge: University Press and Ithaca, N.Y.: Cornell University Press, 1964.

Among many books that review the whole of Wittgenstein's philosophy are:

> George Pitcher, *The Philosophy of Wittgenstein*, Englewood Cliffs, N.J.: Prentice–Hall, 1964.
>
> David Pears, *Wittgenstein*, London: Fontana, 1971.
>
> P. M. S. Hacker, *Insight and Illusion: Wittgenstein on Philosophy and the Metaphysics of Experience*, Oxford: University Press, 1972.

Chapter 9 Ayer

The anthology cited as *LP* is an excellent source of readings. It begins with a good brief history of logical positivism by the editor, ends with a generous bibliography, and includes a number of translations from *Erkenntnis*, the house journal of the movement.

> A. J. Ayer, *Logical Positivism*, New York: Free Press, 1959.

Ayer's *Language, Truth and Logic* brought logical positivism to England when the author was twenty-six. It is still the best brief statement of the position. The following sequence of early books by members of the Vienna Circle gives a deeper understanding of the developments:

Moritz Schlick, *Theory of Knowledge,* Berlin: Springer, 1974 (*Allgemeine Erkenntnislehre,* Berlin: Springer, 1918, 1925).

Rudolf Carnap, *The Logical Structure of the World,* trans. R. A. George, London: Routledge and Kegan Paul, 1967 (*Der Logische Aufbau der Welt,* Berlin: Weltkreis–Verlag, 1928).

Rudolf Carnap, *The Logical Syntax of Language,* London: Kegan Paul, Trubner and Trench and New York: Harcourt Brace, 1937 (*Logische Syntax der Sprache,* Vienna: Springer, 1934).

For a good view of the entire working life of a member of the Circle, see:

The Philosophy of Rudolf Carnap, ed. Paul Schilpp, La Salle, Ill.: Open Court, 1963.

Finally, it is very important to read the work of the philosopher who would always have rejected the title of positivist, and who spurned verificationism from the beginning, but who developed in Vienna, thinking through many of the same philosophical problems and enduring many of the political ones:

Karl Popper, *The Logic of Scientific Discovery,* London: Hutchinson, 1959 (*Logik der Forschung,* Vienna: Springer, 1935).

Chapter 10 Malcolm

Norman Malcolm, *Dreaming,* London: Routledge and Kegan Paul and New York: Humanities Press, 1959.

This book appeared shortly after the modern era of experimental work on dreaming began, in 1953, when Eugene Aserlinsky noticed the periodic eye movements of sleeping infants. Malcolm referred chiefly to a pioneer work:

W. Dement and N. Kleitman, 'The Relation of Eye Movements during Sleep to Dream Activity: An Objective Method for the Study of Dreaming', *Journal of Experimental Psychology,* LIII (1957), 339–46.

A great deal of research has been conducted since then. There are several popular expositions, but all rapidly become out of date:

G. G. Luce and J. Segal, *Sleep,* New York: Coward–McCann, 1966.

Ian Oswald, *Sleep,* Harmondsworth: Penguin, 1970.

Chapter 11 Feyerabend

Characteristic essays of Feyerabend's are:

'Problems of Empiricism', in *Beyond the Edge of Certainty*, ed. R. Colodny (Englewood Cliffs, N.J.: Prentice–Hall, 1965), pp. 145–260.

'Problems of Empiricism II', in *The Nature and Function of Scientific Theories*, ed. R. Colodny (Pittsburgh, Pa.: University of Pittsburgh Press, 1970, pp. 275–354.

'Explanation, Reduction and Empiricism', in *Minnesota Studies in the Philosophy of Science*, III, eds. H. Feigl and G. Maxwell (Minneapolis: University of Minnesota Press, 1962), pp. 28–97.

'Against Method', *ibid.* IV, eds. M. Radner and S. Winokur, 1970, pp. 17–130.

'Philosophy of Science, a Subject with a Great Past', *ibid.* V, ed. R. H. Steuwer, 1970, pp. 172–83.

The 'Pittsburgh series' edited by Colodny and the *Minnesota Studies* include many articles on similar topics. The work of Kuhn, Hanson, and Lakatos is essential collateral reading:

Thomas Kuhn, *The Structure of Scientific Revolutions*, Chicago: University of Chicago Press, 1962.

N. R. Hanson, *Patterns of Discovery*, Cambridge: University Press, 1958.

Imre Lakatos, 'Falsification and the Methodology of Research Programmes', in *Criticism and the Growth of Knowledge*, eds. I. Lakatos and A. Musgrave (Cambridge: University Press, 1970), pp. 91–196.

This last anthology is a reconstruction of a conference that occurred in 1965, and has a valuable debate involving Kuhn, Feyerabend, Lakatos, Popper, and others. For a major earlier work by Lakatos, see:

'Proofs and refutations', *British Journal for the Philosophy of Science*, XIV (1963), 1–25, 120–39, 221–45, 296–342. An edition of his work, including much unpublished material, is in preparation.

Chapter 12 Davidson

This is a selection of Davidson's chief papers on language, together with some of his more important articles on action, causation, and events. Items marked * seem particularly useful. The list is long because no such list can otherwise be readily obtained.

*"Action Reasons, and Causes', *The Journal of Philosophy*, LX (1963), 685–700.

'The Method of Extension and Intension', in *The Philosophy of Rudolf Carnap*, ed. P. Schilpp (La Salle, Ill.: Open Court, 1963), pp. 311–50.

'Theories of Meaning and Learnable Languages', in *Logic Methodology and Philosophy of Science: Proceedings of the 1964 International Congress* (Amsterdam, 1965), pp. 383–94.

*'The Logical Form of Action Sentences', in *The Logic of Decision and Action*, ed. N. Rescher (Pittsburgh, Pa.: University of Pittsburgh Press, 1967), pp. 81–120.

*'Truth and Meaning', *Synthese*, VII (1967), 304–23.

'Causal Relations', *The Journal of Philosophy*, LXIV (1967), 691–703.

*'True to the Facts', *ibid*. LXVI (1969), 158–74.

'On Events and Event Descriptions', in *Facts and Existence*, ed. J. Margolis (Oxford: Blackwell, 1969), pp. 74–84.

'On Saying That', in *Words and Objections*, eds. D. Davidson and J. Hintikka (Dordrecht: Reidel, 1969), pp. 158–74.

'Action and Reaction', *Inquiry*, XIII (1970), 140–8.

'Events as Particulars', *Nous*, IV (1970), 25–32.

'The Individuation of Events', in *Essays in Honor of Carl Hempel*, ed. N. Rescher (Dordrecht: Reidel, 1970), pp. 216–34.

'Agency', in *Agent, Action and Reason*, ed. R. Binkley (Toronto: University of Toronto Press, 1971), pp. 3–25.

'Mental Events', in *Experience and Theory*, eds. L. Foster and J. Swanson (Boston: Belknap, 1971), pp. 79–101.

'In Defence of Convention T', in *Truth, Syntax and Modality*, ed. H. Leblanc (Amsterdam: North Holland, 1973), 76–85.

'Semantics for Natural Languages', in *Linguaggi nella Società e nella Tecnica* (Milan: Edizione di Comunità, 1970), pp. 177–88.

Chapter 13 Why Does Language Matter?

H. P. Grice's work on meaning is best represented by the following three articles:

'Meaning', *The Philosophical Review*, LXVI (1957), 377–88; reprinted in *Philosophical Logic*, ed. P. F. Strawson, Oxford: University Press, 1967.

'Utterer's Meaning and Intentions', *ibid*. LXXVIII (1969), 147–77.

'Utterer's Meaning, Sentence Meaning, and Word Meaning', *Foundations of Language*, IV (1968), 225–42; reprinted in *The Philosophy of Language*, ed. J. Searle, Oxford: University Press, 1971.

Some aspects of his theory are elaborated in:

    Stephen Schiffer, *Meaning*, Oxford: University Press, 1973.

    J. F. Bennett, 'The Meaning–Nominalist Strategy', *Foundations of Language*, x (1973), 141–68.

Bennett is now completing a book that develops many of the themes in his article.

Karl Popper's most famous book is the first on the following list, but the other works round out his interests:

    The Logic of Scientific Discovery, London: Hutchinson, 1958 (an augmented translation of *Logik der Forschung*, Vienna: Springer, 1935).

    Conjectures and Refutations, London: Hutchinson, 1963.

    Objective Knowledge: An Evolutionary Approach, Oxford: University Press, 1972.

    The Philosophy of Karl Popper, 2 vols., ed. P. A. Schilpp, La Salle, Ill.: Open Court, 1974.

Index

abstractionism, 59, 64
acids, 110–12, 115f, 122
acupuncture, 124
adverbs, 137–9
Alston, W. 18f, 43, 72
Althusser, L., 185–7
Anscombe, G.E.M., 30
Archimedes, 162
Aristotle, 31, 68, 73, 82, 161, 186
Armstrong, D., 27f
Arnauld, A., 26, 108, 165
articulation, 86
Austin, J.L., 2, 8, 135
Ayer, A.J., 92–102, 172

Babel, 88
Bacon, F., 4, 17, 186
Bedeutung, 49-51.
Bennett, J., 44–9, 94
Berkeley, G., 2, 16f, 26, 34–42,
    63, 71, 76, 84, 86, 115, 163f,
    182, 185
Berlin, I., 99f
blank slate, 58
Borges, G., 27
Boyle, R., 34
British Association, 166
Buffier, C., 85, 88

Caesar, Julius, 47f
Campbell, N. 118–28
Carnap, R., 96–102, 120
charity, 146–58
Chomsky, N., 2, 26, 57–69, 84,
    90–2, 111, 136–7

Church, A., 100f
common acceptation, 47, 76
Condorcet, M.J.A.N.C., 164
concept (Campbell) 123
Condillac, 164
consistency, 135f
Convention T, 132–56
Copenhagen interpretation, 125,
    178
copula, 88
corpuscular philosophy, 34f
Cook, Captain, 150
critical philosophy, 93, 107
crucial experiments, 117f, 123f,
    178

Dalton, J., 111, 116
Davidson, D., 89, 91, 128,
    129–56, 161, 179
decision theory, 146f
Deleuze, G., 10
demarcation, Popper's problem,
    96
Derrida, J., 10
Descartes, R. 8, 30–6, 40, 46,
    60f, 64, 104, 108, 160–2
descriptions, theory of 78, 89
Destutt de Tracy, 164, 167
determinism, 5
Dilthey, W., 153, 168, 171
discourse, 52, 104, 159, 164, 167,
    180f, 187
dreaming, 8, 103–12, 177
Dummett, M.A.E., 180f

ego, Cartesian, 11, 38, 46, 104, 159, 164, 169, 182
Einstein, A., 125
epistemology, 166
Euclid, 37, 62, 162
existential commitment, 29f

facts, 84, 131
family resemblance, 38f
Febvre, L., 32, 152
Fermat, P., 117
Feyerabend, P., 9, 115–28, 152, 161, 178–80
Foucault, M., 10, 27f, 30, 32, 84, 187
free will, 4f
Frege, G., 49–53, 57, 72, 79f, 122f, 141, 166, 170, 173, 177, 180
Freud, S., 51, 96, 124

games, 38f
Geach, P.T., 3, 59, 64
Gentzen, G., 39
geometry, 37–9
George III, 183
Gödel, K., 139
Goodman, N. 64–9
grammar, 66, 81, 85, 90, 136
Grandy, R., 149
Grant, U.S., 60
Grice, H.P., 20f, 148, 180
grue/bleen, 65f

Hanson, N.R., 120, 163
Hartley, D., 3
Hegel, G.W.F., 168, 185–7
Heidegger, M., 96, 100
Hempel, C.G., 101f, 112, 161, 176
Hilbert, D., 63
Hobbes, T., 2, 5, 15–25, 163f, 181
holism, 131
humanity, principle of, 146–50
Hume, D., 2, 3, 163, 168f, 176, 183
Husserl, E., 171

idea, 11–12
  abstract, 37–9
  identity of 44f
  innate 57–69, 90
  Port Royal 15–25, 83
  heyday of, 163–10, 172, 185
idealism, 17, 35–42, 84, 174, 182
idéologues, 164, 183
imprinting, 68
incommensurable theories, 124, 152f
intentions, 20f, 180

James, W. 5
Jansenism, 26

'kangaroo', 150
Kant, I., 28, 39, 93, 106, 168, 170, 183
knowing subject, 159, 182, 187
Kripke, S., 79
Kuhn, T.S., 124

Lakatos, I., 126
Leibniz, G.W., 31, 57f, 64, 93, 104, 162, 165
lingualism (linguistic idealism) 89f, 174, 182
linguistics, 3, 4, 90
Locke, J., 2, 6–8, 19, 26f, 30, 34, 39, 44–54, 58f, 64, 71, 76, 80, 163f, 167
logical atomism, 72-81, 174f
logical form, 81–90, 137

Mach, E., 51, 179
McLuhan, M., 186
Malcolm, N., 8, 103–12, 172, 175, 177
Malebranche, 26, 32, 165
marble block (Leibniz) 58
March! 24
marigolds, 44, 73, 86–9, 102
Mark Anthony, 47
Marx, K., 96, 164
matter, 6, 34f
meaning, theories of ,
  pure and applied, 1–7

ideational, referential and
   behavioural, 18–24
   defined, 49–53
   death of, 128, 180
Mill, James, 2
Mill, John Stuart, 2, 15, 26
Montague, R. 139
Moore, G.E., 2, 71
Mundle, C.W.K., 8

name,
   in Hobbes, 18
   logically proper, 77–81
Napoleon, 164, 183
Newton, I., 35, 125
Nicole, P., 26
Nietzsche, F., 176
Nixon, R., 183
nominalism, 141

object, and subject reversal,
   30–33, in *Tractatus*, 89
Ogden, C.K., 171
Oxford linguistic philosophy, 9

Pears, D., 71
Penny's barbecue, 19
personal identity, 169
Peters, R., 23
phenomenology, 171
Pitcher, G., 8
Plato, 38f, 62, 103f, 121, 157,
   186
Popper, K., 95–8, 184–7
poppies, 64
Port Royal, 26–33, 85, 159, 167,
   170
possible worlds, 140
presupposition, 3
private language, 8, 76, 173, 180
Putnam, H., 110–12, 115, 177
Pythagoras, 63

qualities, primary and secondary,
   34f
quantum mechanics, 117, 125,
   178

Quine, W. van O., 9, 65, 80f, 145,
   150–5, 159f, 177–80, 184

rain, 36f
rapid eye movements (REM),
   109–12, 115
Rawls, J., 25
reference, 46–51
Reid, T., 163f, 169, 176
relativity theory, 125
Richards, I. A., 171
Roosevelt, F.D., 72
Russell, B., 3, 4, 19, 70–90, 94,
   137, 172–5

satisfaction, 134
Schlick, M., 94–102, 106
scientia, 161
sense (*Sinn*) 49
sense data, 77, 89, 175
sign, 18–25, 35, 46
Sinn, 49f, 57, 68, 141, 166, 170
Snell's law, 117f
Socrates, 62, 78, 103f, 172
speculative philosophy, 93
Spinoza, 7, 131, 185
Stalin, 72, 75, 77–80, 173
Stallo, J.B., 51
stimulus meaning, 151, 155
stimulus–response model, 3, 124
Strawson, P.F., 3, 9, 79f, 83, 94,
   183
structure, deep and surface, 90
Stutz Bearcat, 60
subject–predicate logic, 70, 80, 89
substance, 70, 80f, 91

Tarski, A., 130–7, 154
theory-laden terms, 120f
tomato chutney, 29
translation, 44, 101f, 112,
   118–20, 140–57
   radical, 145
   indeterminacy of, 151–6
truth, 84, 130–57

underdetermination, 65, 91
universals, 37f, 73, 89, 175

validity, 82
Ventris, M., 148
verification, 94–112, 175, 177
Verstehen, 153
Vienna Circle, 94–102, 120, 175,
177–80
vision, 31–3, 159

Warnock, G., 27

Weber, M., 51, 153, 170
Whewell, W., 166, 176
Wilson, N.L., 147f
Winch, P., 153
Wisdom, J.O., 34
Wittgenstein, L., 2, 8, 17, 24, 38,
68, 88f, 92, 102, 153, 172–7,
182